INSIGHT COMPACT GUIDES

ROME

GREAT LITTLE GUIDES

Insight Compact Guide: Rome is a culture-based guide for one of the most cultured cities in Europe. It details all the ancient Roman monuments, the museum collections and all the delights of its streets and squares.

This is just one title in *Apa Publications'* new series of pocket-sized, easy-to-use guidebooks intended for the independent-minded traveller. Based on an established, award-winning formula pioneered in Germany, *Insight Compact Guides* pride themselves on being up-to-date and authoritative. They are in essence mini travel encyclopedias, designed to be comprehensive yet portable, both readable and reliable.

D0381354

Star Attractions

An instant reference to some of Rome's most popular tourist attractions to help you on your way.

Pantheon p21

Roman Forum p28

Trevi Fountain p43

Colosseum p52

St Peter's p54

Pietà p56

The Vatican p59

Raphael rooms p63

Sistine Chapel p65

Castel Sant'Angelo p75

Villa d'Este p78

Rome

Introduction

Places

Culture

Leisure

Practical Information

Rome – The Eternal City

Opposite: Classical columns, Forum Romanum

The city conjures up the famous saying, 'All roads lead to Rome' – which of course they once did. As the capital of the Roman Empire, Rome attracted many different peoples from the ancient world, and as the centre of Christianity until the present day, the city has lost none of its cosmopolitan appeal. In ancient times, Rome was seen as the centre of the world, ruler of an empire stretching from Gaul and Spain in the west to Egypt and Asia Minor in the east.

View from San Pietro, Trastevere

The city's urban design and architectural history can be closely studied in each phase of development. A walk or bus ride from Trastevere through the historic centre reveals Rome as one of the most legible cities. From Trastevere's Ponte Garibaldi stretch views of Isola Tiberina, the sacred island, with a Roman bridge leading to the Jewish ghetto; on the far bank of the Tiber are picturesque palaces and the Teatro Argentina quarter, with the remains of four temples; beyond is the Pantheon, the best preserved Roman temple of all; further east lies the Colosseum, the grandest amphitheatre in the world. Welcome to Rome.

5

Location and size

Rome is on the same line of latitude as New York. As well as being the capital of Italy, Rome is capital of the sparsely populated region of Latium (Lazio) and of the Province of Rome. The city is built on seven legendary hills: the Capitoline, Palatine, Aventine, Esquiline, Viminale, Quirinale and Celio (Caelian). The City of Rome (Comune di Roma) occupies 1,507sq km (581sq miles), of which the Vatican City takes up 44 ha (108 acres).

Northern Lazio features wooded hills with volcanic lakes and the Apennines beyond. Southwestern Lazio includes the monotonous Pontine marshes. To the southeast lie the Colli Albani (Alban Hills), a district of cool lakes, charming towns (Castelli Romani) and wine-growing slopes. The yellow Tiber (Tevere) is the major river, with its source to the southwest of San Marino in the Apennines; it flows into the Province of Rome via the hills to the north of the city, then through the city itself and, 35km (22 miles) further on, runs into the sea near Ostia, the commercial port of ancient Rome.

The glory of ancient Rome

The She-wolf with Romulus and Remus

The citizens of pre-Christian Rome could already look back over a thousand years of history, from the first days of the Roman Republic to the fall of the Roman Empire. Coins minted during the period of imperial decline extol the glory of the city: Rome is referred to as *Roma dea*, 'Rome, the goddess'.

Pax romana spelt stability and prosperity, with Roman citizenship a ticket to success. The people were mollified by a clever policy summed up by Juvenal as 'bread and circuses', bribes ranging from the provision of free food to such popular spectacles as riotous chariot-racing and bloody gladiatorial combat. Circus Maximus, the oldest and largest stadium, is today an oval, grassy esplanade. The baroque Piazza Navona was once Domitian's Stadium, the site of a first-century stadium, used for Roman athletic games.

Rome has weathered all the storms of history from the 8th century BC to the present day, and is worthy of its title: *Roma Eterna*, 'the Eternal City'. Aqua Traiana, the underground aqueduct built during the rule of Emperor Trajan, still carries water to Rome from Lake Bracciano. The ancient streets extend from the centre of the city in star formation, with the old routes and names preserved to this day.

The famous Via Appia, or Appian Way, lined by family tombs (*see page 38*), leaves the city to the south; it was the route taken by travellers heading for Brindisi, Taranto and eventually Greece. Via Aurelia left Rome to the west and led up the Tyrrhenian coast as far as Ventimiglia and the former province of Gallia; Via Cassia led to Florence via Viterbo and Siena; Via Flaminia through Umbria, and to Rimini on the Adriatic; Via Salaria also led to the Adriatic, past Rieti, as did Via Tiburtina, which ran to Pescara. Today's Autostrada del Sole to Naples follows the course of the ancient Via Casilina.

A citizen of Rome

Temple of the Faustina, Villa Borghese Park

The Roman spell

Rome has been an artistic holiday playground since time immemorial. In the 17th century, the Roman landscape was painted in heroic style by French artists Nicolas Poussin and Claude Lorrain; 18th-century Englishmen on the Grand Tour flocked to the atmospheric ruins; poets like Byron, Shelley and Keats found freedom from English conservatism.

For today's traveller, there are hundreds of additional reasons to visit the Eternal City. Rome is an artistic treasure house, with museums cluttered with Renaissance and Roman exhibits. Dotted through the city are medieval churches filled with magnificent mosaics, made of glass, multi-coloured marble and stone. After a surfeit of high culture in stifling heat, a retreat to the lush gardens of Villa Borghese provides a chance to relax – and to spot languid Romans at play.

The Vatican City, still an independent City State, is one of the world's most visited sights. As the seat of the Papacy, it is still the Roman Catholic Mecca, with its jewel, St Peter's, the largest church in Christendom. The Vatican's spiritual subjects are estimated at over 900 million, about 20 per cent of the world's population. The Vatican museums are amongst the most splendid in the world, with Etruscan, Roman and Renaissance exhibits, culminating in Michelangelo's fabulously frescoed Sistine Chapel (*see page 65*). Yet despite the presence of the Vatican and of 400 churches in the historic centre alone, the Romans are not noted for their piety. As local wisdom has it: 'Faith is made here but believed elsewhere.'

The impact of Roman civilisation is immeasurable, not merely in religious life. The Roman model is at the heart of many of our political and legal systems, and the Latin language has had a lasting influence. Indeed, we owe it such concepts as 'citizens', 'civic', 'nepotism', 'plebeian' and 'pontificate'. Democracy and civic life have been greatly enriched by Rome.

In the field of architecture, Rome rivals ancient Greece as the trail-blazer of the Western world. Triumphal arches and imperial villas are Rome's greatest gift to architecture but the city's functional apartment blocks (*insulae*) represent the concept closest to the modern mind. Rome is rich in atmospheric ruins, including public baths, temples, tombs, catacombs, mausoleums, obelisks, aqueducts and stretches of ancient Roman roads. The public fountains, adorned with Classical motifs, are still one of the glories of Rome. Over a thousand grace the city, with the most stunning on Piazza di Trevi and Piazza Navona. The splendour of ancient Roman architecture may be due to civic munificence, but many of the finest churches, fountains and palazzi are a legacy of papal patronage. As a result of such fortune, the city offers buildings spanning several millennia.

7

Street scene

However, contemporary Rome has also been shaped by its recent past. Around the turn of the century, various monumental structures were created, such as the Victor Emmanuel Monument (Il Vittoriano), the buildings of the Italian Fascists between the two World Wars, as well as the postwar residential area known as EUR (*see page 87*) with its grandiose Palazzo dello Sport.

Rome today

Outsiders see modern-day Rome as the pulsating heart of the Italian Republic, which in many ways it is. To most Italians, however, the capital is perceived as a parasite with a bloated bureaucracy and a history of inefficiency and political corruption; this also is partly true. Yet for all its problems, the city is vital, resilient, easy-going, a truly human capital.

Today Rome boasts a population of almost four million, only four times the population of ancient Rome in its heyday. According to Alberto Moravia, Rome's greatest

Palazzo del Quirinale parade

Waiting for customers

modern novelist, 'There are no Romans, only people from other parts of Italy who have adopted Roman characteristics.' This may be true but Rome's genius has always been to meld disparate peoples into a cohesive whole, forming highly civilised citizens, imbued with civic pride.

Rome is divided into 22 districts (*rioni*) within the Aurelian Wall, with an additional 41 *quartieri* outside the historic city; and six suburbs (*borgate*). Noisy traffic crawls through the complex network of medieval streets in the city's *centro storico* (historic centre). Yet Rome is also a city for pedestrians and needs to be discovered on foot. Strollers will be rewarded by stunning views and vistas: a narrow alley may suddenly open on to a bustling market such as Campo de' Fiori, or reveal somewhere as theatrical as Piazza Navona.

Contemporary Rome has made a name for itself as a shopping mecca. As well as vibrant markets, there are idiosyncratic specialist shops for hand-crafted ceramics, prints, antiques, stylish furniture and designer fashion. The sheer variety of elegant boutiques in Via Condotti, with a view of the grandiose Spanish Steps, is rivalled only by the range of cuisine on offer.

Roman taste is gutsy and proletarian, with the emphasis on roasted vegetable *antipasti* (hors d'oeuvres), sweetbreads, seafood pasta and the famous *saltimbocca alla romana* (veal with parma ham). Eating out in Rome can be a superb experience, ranging from tiny *trattorie* in the narrow streets of Trastevere to sophisticated restaurants on chic Via Veneto.

Traffic and pollution are major urban concerns but an environmentally-minded mayor, elected in 1993, is trying to tackle the situation. Under discussion is a controversial plan to transform the Forum area into a pedestrian precinct and to remove Mussolini's Via dei Fori Imperiali. The resulting archaeological park would be unique and in keeping with the city's cultural heritage. However, with its romantic ruins and labyrinthine historic centre, Rome already promises countless archaeological adventures.

The best time of year to visit Rome is in the spring or late summer; at the height of summer it is often stifling, while in winter it tends to rain a great deal. Yet summer has its compensations: music recitals in charming medieval churches; opera or ballet in the Roman Baths of Caracalla; jazz sessions in the grounds of Villa Doria Pamphili; and Festa de' Noiantri, the boisterous Trastevere street festival. Rome has a festival for every season, with one of the most colourful being the Spanish Steps in Bloom. In April and May, the steps are draped with a red carpet and hung with tubs of bright pink azaleas; the steps are soon transformed into a stage for a spontaneous Roman spectacle.

Ancient Rome

The city's origins

The legend of Rome's foundation – whereby the shepherd Faustulus abandoned the twins Romulus and Remus in a basket, and they were then reared by a she-wolf – cannot be historically proven. However, the traditional date of 753BC does concur with the urbanisation of Latium (present-day Lazio) during the 8th century BC. At the ford across the Tiber, the north-south route from Etruria to Campagna intersected with an important salt-trading route that led inland from the coast; this provided ideal conditions for Rome's later development.

Roma quadrata is traditionally regarded as the heart of the settlement, and its remains can be seen on the Palatine (*see page 30*). This 'town' grew very quickly, however, and expanded to include the surrounding hills. The Forum, situated on the outskirts of the town on the Palatine, was originally a necropolis (*see page 26*), but as the town expanded it gradually developed into a residential area, and the cemetery was eventually shifted to the Esquiline. Archaeological evidence shows that this early Rome had trading links with the Greek colonies in Southern Italy. Thanks to its mercantile power it was soon the dominant economic force in Latium.

Rome's seven legendary kings

By the early 6th century BC the Etruscans – who probably came originally from Asia Minor – had achieved cultural and political hegemony in the area occupied by present-day Tuscany to the north. According to ancient sources a certain Tarquinius Priscus, of Etruscan origin, ruled over Rome in 616BC. He was one of the legendary seven kings who ruled the city until 510BC; during his reign Rome was given its first fortifications. The marshland in the valley between the Capitoline, Palatine and Esquiline was reclaimed in 575BC with the aid of the *Cloaca Maxima*, a remarkable drainage system, while the second to last of the seven kings, Servius Tullius, is believed to have built the city's first wall (11km/7 miles long) in the 6th century BC; impressive remains of this Servian Wall can be seen at the Stazione Termini (*see page 45*).

The Roman Republic

The Etruscan 'Rome of the Tarquins' ended with the expulsion of King Tarquinius Superbus in roughly 510BC; the Romans must thus have founded their own republic around this time. This new Republic was headed by two consuls, who were changed annually, and a high priest. During the century that followed, the Republic attempted to defend its hold on Latium against the attacks of neighbouring powers. The Romans gradually advanced into territory in present-day Tuscany that had formerly been held by the Etruscans. The defeat of the Etruscans of Veio in 396BC was then followed by a setback for Rome in 387BC when it was attacked by the Gauls. The latter were successfully repelled, however, and the old Servian city wall was rebuilt in around 377BC.

Rome's perpetual internal conflicts between the patricians and the plebeians now came to a head, and the year 366BC saw the first appointment of a plebeian as consul. The Roman Republic's long struggles to survive had cut it off from its earlier north-south trading routes; a trade agreement with Carthage marked a new beginning in 348BC, and the Samnite Wars (which lasted until 290BC) confirmed Roman supremacy in Central Italy. In 326BC the Greek colony of *Neapolis* (today's Naples) joined forces with Rome, and *Perusia* (Perugia) fell in 309BC. By 290BC the Samnites, Etruscans and Umbrians had all been defeated, and Rome was doing battle with the Greeks. *Tarentum* (Taranto) fell in 272BC, and the rest of Central and Southern Italy thus became Roman. The Republic now began to expand beyond the confines of the Italian mainland.

Rome's colonies

The fierce battle for Sicily was won during the course of the three Punic Wars; Rome continued to expand. By 238BC it had taken Sicily, Corsica and Sardinia; by 201BC Syracuse and the eastern and southern coasts of Spain; by 133BC the rest of Northern Italy, Spain, Greece, Western Asia Minor and Carthage. In that same year the political and social conflicts at the heart of the Republic led to civil war; the reformer Tiberius Gracchus met with opposition from the landowning nobility, and the superiority of the Senate was gradually reinstated. The conflicts grew worse, however, and finally led to the end of the Republic in 31BC. During the last century BC the great names of Roman history made their appearance: Marius and Sulla, Cicero and Catilina, Pompey and Crassus, Cato, Caesar and Octavian, who as Augustus became the city's first emperor in 31BC and assumed control of an empire that stretched from the Mediterranean and the Black Sea to Gaul and Britain.

Historical Highlights

31BC–AD14 Augustus founds the Empire and establishes peace. The arts flourish, especially in Rome. Roads are built to the furthest extremities of the Empire, and even today Roman milestones can be found in Spain and Scotland, along the Euphrates and near Carthage.

AD64 After setting fire to Rome, Nero builds his famous 'Golden House'.

69–79 Vespasian has the Flavian Amphitheatre built; it is later renamed the Colosseum. The Arch of Titus is erected in the Forum to commemorate the emperor's son Titus's destruction of Jerusalem in ad70.

98–117 The Roman Empire achieves its greatest territorial expansion under emperor Trajan. It extends as far as the East Frisian islands to the north, Mesopotamian lands to the east, the whole of North Africa to the south and Spain and Britain to the west. The arts flourish not only in Rome, but also in the colonies.

117–38 Hadrian secures the borders of the empire by building walls. His burial place is today's Castel Sant'Angelo.

161–80 Marcus Aurelius. The column of Marcus Aurelius, with reliefs showing his victories over Danubian tribes, still stands today in Rome's Piazza Colonna.

193–211 Septimius Severus. The triumphal arch in the Forum named after him commemorates his victories over the Parthians.

250 First persecution of the Christians under the emperor Decius.

284–305 Diocletian. During his reign the Empire begins its decline; he introduces the tetrarchy, whereby four persons share power simultaneously. Renewed persecution of the Christians.

312 Constantine defeats Maxentius near the Milvian Bridge across the Tiber. Christianity officially recognised. In 330 Byzantium, now Constantinople, becomes the official capital of the Empire.

395 The Roman Empire is finally divided once and for all. Ninety years later, in 404, Ravenna becomes the capital of the Western part.

410 Rome captured by the invading Visigoths under King Alaric.

455 Rome plundered by the Vandals.

476 Fall of the Western Roman Empire. Power is now assumed by the Germans: first by Odoacer, then by Theodoric, king of the Ostrogoths.

536 Rome captured by Byzantium. East Roman rule in Italy re-established.

590–604 Pope Gregory the Great protects Rome from further pillaging by making peace with the Lombards (593).

756 Pepin the Short, king of the Franks, comes to the aid of Pope Stephen III, returns to the church the lands taken from it by the Lombards, and lays the foundation of the temporal sovereignty of the popes (Papal States) by giving the pope the exarchate of Ravenna.

800 Pope Leo III crowns Charlemagne emperor in St Peter's. The Roman Empire is restored in name.

12th century An insurrection, which is led by the churchman Arnold of Brescia, takes place during the papacy of Adrian IV (Nicholas Breakspear, the only English Pope). Arnold of Brescia is executed in 1155.

1309 Clement V removes the seat of the papacy to Avignon in the south of France. The so-called 'second Babylonian captivity' of the popes begins.

1377 Gregory XI returns to Rome. The resulting 'western schism' within the church is finally extinguished only in 1417 with the election of Pope Martin V.

Rome undergoes a new phase of prosperity during the Renaissance and again becomes the capital of the known world. The Popes attract famous artists to Rome to have their city, and especially the Vatican, decorated. They include Bellini, Botticelli, Bramante, Donatello, Leonardo da Vinci, Michelangelo, Palladio, Raphael and Titian.

1527 Charles V's army sacks Rome *(Sacco di Roma)*. The city recovers only very gradually from the devastation inflicted on it.

1585–90 Rome receives a whole new series of fine buildings under Pope Sixtus V. He commissions architects Fontana, Bernini, Borromini and Maderna to build magnificent churches, palaces, squares and fountains.

This brief period of prosperity is followed by a steady decline in Rome's political, cultural and economic importance. The Italian peninsula splits up into numerous smaller states, among them the Papal States, with Rome as their capital. Only Italian unification, which starts in Turin in 1859, leads to a new period of prosperity for Rome.

1798–9 Rome becomes a French-style republic. Pope Pius VI dies in French captivity in 1799.

1801 Pope Pius VII concludes a concordat with Napoleon in order to preserve the independence of Rome and of the Papal States. Rome becomes part of the French Empire under Napoleon's son. In 1814 the Papal States are restored to Pius VII at the Congress of Vienna.

1848 Pope Pius IX gives the Papal States a constitution but refuses to intercede for Italian unification. He is forced to flee and is able to return to Rome only in 1850.

1870 Rome and the Papal States are conquered. In 1871 Rome becomes the capital of the new kingdom of Italy. From now on the Popes live as prisoners in the Vatican.

1922 Benito Mussolini assumes power in Italy, naming his party the Fascisti after the fasces (rods), the symbol of a magistrate's authority in ancient Rome. Broad streets are built alongside many monumental new buildings. Suburbs are built on the outskirts of the city, most of them residential, eg Testaccio and the better known eur.

1929 The Lateran Treaty is signed between the Italian state and the Vatican, making the latter an independent sovereign state with the Pope as its head. The Vatican state also has some additional possessions alongside Vatican City, for example, the Lateran Palace, Santa Maria Maggiore, San Paolo fuori le Mura and the papal summer residence of Castel Gandolfo.

1943 The king has Mussolini placed under arrest. The Allies land in southern Italy. The king and the government leave Rome.

1944 The Allies liberate Rome on 4 June.

1945 Mussolini is hanged in Milan.

1946 After a referendum, Italy decides to become a republic. Rome remains the capital, and King Umberto II is exiled to Portugal.

1957 The European Economic Community (now the European Union) is established by the Treaty of Rome signed by six European nations.

1960 The XVII Olympic Summer Games are held in Rome.

1962 Pope John XXIII opens the Second Vatican Council, which lasts until 1965.

1978 Aldo Moro, Italy's prime minister and the head of the Christian Democrat Party, is kidnapped by the Red Brigade terrorist organisation and murdered. Cardinal Karol Wojtyla from Krakow becomes the first ever Polish pope and assumes the name John Paul II.

1981 The Turk Ali Agca makes an assasination attempt on the pontiff in St Peter's Square; John Paul II survives.

1992 Pope John Paul II officially withdraws the church's 1633 condemnation of Galileo Galilei and his Copernican view of the world.

1993 Italy gains a governmental national unity, a reputable coalition headed by President Scalfaro and Premier Ciampi. Guilio Andreotti, Roman power-broker and seven times Italian premier, is investigated for Mafia association. The investigations of the Milan Department of Public Prosecution into Italy's bribery and corruption scandal (watchword Mani Pulite – clean hands) reach all the way to Rome; in July the other side replies by detonating bombs inside the churches of San Giovanni in Laterano and San Giorgio in Velabro.

1994 National elections usher in a new Italian Republic, an electoral system modelled along British 'first-past-the-post' lines. Silvio Berlusconi, a media magnate, is the new premier.

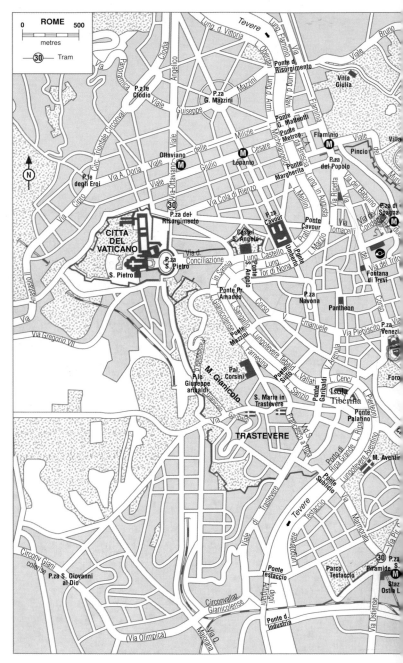

Victor Emmanuel Monument

Preceding pages:
St Peter's Square

Selling jewellery on the street

Mussolini Balcony,
Palazzo Venezia

Route 1

★ Piazza Venezia – ★ Largo Argentina – ★ Campo de'Fiori – ★★ Piazza Navona – ★★★ Pantheon – Piazza della Minerva – ★ Piazza Sant'Ignazio – ★ Piazza Colonna – ★ Piazza San Silvestro – Corso – Via Condotti – ★ Spanish Steps

Towering above the ★ Piazza Venezia is the enormous **Victor Emmanuel Monument ❶**, built in 1911 to symbolise the achievement of Italian unity (1870) and in honour of Italy's first king, who died in 1878. This colossal monument (135m/440ft wide, 130m/425ft long, 70m/230ft high) contains an Altar to the Fatherland as well as the grave of Italy's Unknown Soldier. The building's architectural worth is still the subject of much dispute, with several voices in Rome calling for the 'typewriter' (Rome's word for the monument) to be removed.

The ★ **Palazzo Venezia ❷**, which gave this five-way intersection its name, was a papal residence briefly, then the embassy of the Venetian Republic (1564–1797); later it became the Austrian embassy, and it was occupied by Mussolini during the Fascist regime. Today the building (1452–91) houses the Museo di Palazzo Venezia and also the State Institute of Art History and Archaeology. The severe, fortress-like Renaissance facade with its battlements still betrays the building's original defensive function. Integrated into it as a kind of palace chapel, as it were, is the Church of San Marco, which dates back to the 4th century, though it received its present-day appearance in the 15th century: a basilica with a pillared portico, with a mag-

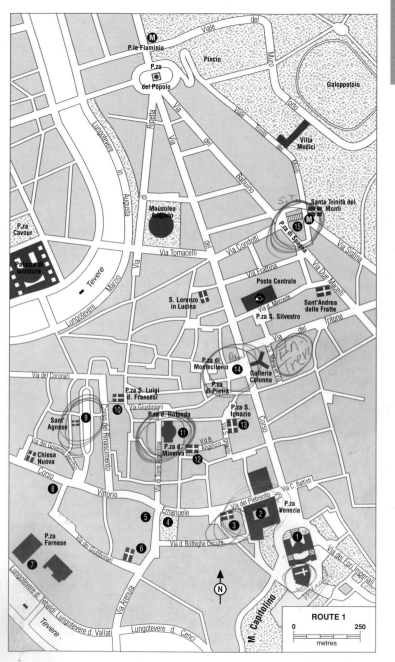

nificent coffered ceiling and also some 9th-century mosaics in its apse. Next to the church is the delightful interior courtyard of the Palazzo Venezia, almost like an oasis with its two-storeyed arcade, luxuriant foliage, and baroque fountain with statues representing Venezia and the lion of St Mark. Back in the square it's worth taking a look at the Romanesque campanile; it dates from the 12th century, and was one of the first to be built in the city.

From the Piazza Venezia the Via del Plebiscito leads off westwards to the Piazza del Gesù, which is dominated by the mighty facade of the church of **Il Gesù ❸**. This early baroque facade, which dates from 1575, was a model for many later imitations. St Ignatius Loyola, the founder of the Jesuit Order, died in very humble circumstances on the site of this Jesuit church, which also has a magnificent baroque interior. The exterior was designed by Giacomo Della Porta, built by Vignola and financed by Cardinal Alessandro Farnese. The main entrance to the central aisle is at the centre of the two-storeyed facade. The architecture here is a symbolic representation of the centralised power structure of the baroque period. The interior of the church is also expressive of this concentration on the omnipotence of the Lord of Heaven; the huge barrel vault and the fresco of the *Triumph of the Name of Jesus*, with its superb foreshortening effects, make the heavens actually appear to be opening.

Ceiling of Il Gesù, by Bacicca

This and other frescoes by Baciccia from Genoa in the aisle, dome and apse were painted only in 1669, a full century after the building was completed, when the Jesuits' struggles to reform the Catholic Church were already over. This explains the stark contrast between the building's architectural clarity and its over-elaborate decoration, the result of later centuries. The high altar dates from 1834–43 and is neoclassical; the chapel to the left of it, Santa Maria degli Astalli, contains a fine early 15th-century altar painting taken from the church of the same name which formerly stood on the site. The Jesuit Andrea del Pozzo built the ★ **Cappella di Sant'Ignazio di Loyola** (1696–1700) in the left transept; the grave of the saint lies beneath it.

The ★★ **altar** is considered the most valuable in the Christian world, being decorated with gold, bronze, lapis lazuli, marble and alabaster. The terrestrial globe being carried by the angels is actually the largest block of lapis lazuli in existence. The statue of the saint was formerly of solid silver; it was melted down in 1797 and presented to Napoleon as tribute; today's statue, a copy, is only silver-plated. The artistic value of the marble groups to the left and right of the altar remains an object of controversy; like the *Trinity* on the gable, they are 18th-century creations. The balustrade in front of the altar is also particularly fine.

The Via del Plebiscito leads into the Corso Vittorio Emanuele II, one of Rome's largest thoroughfares; between the two streets lie the ruins of the ★ **Area Sacra Argentina ❹**. Four temples dating from Rome's days as a republic were unearthed here between 1926 and 1930, and their outlines – one of them is round – can still be easily made out. The oldest of them, situated a little further down, has been dated to 300BC, and is thus one of the most ancient monuments in the city. One of the oldest theatres is the **Teatro Argentina ❺**, opened in 1731, where the first performance of Rossini's *Barber of Seville* was given in 1816.

The Via Arenula leads towards the River Tiber, and branching off it, at the Piazza Cairoli, is the Via dei Giubbonari. Here we come to the church of **San Carlo ai Catinari ❻**, one of the three churches in Rome consecrated to San Carlo Borromeo, a saint who fought for the reform of the Roman Catholic faith in the 16th century. The ground-plan of this church is a Greek cross; the dome was built by Rosati between 1611 and 1620. The magnificent facade dates from 1635; the interior decoration is rather mediocre in contrast.

The Via dei'Giubbonari, which has become a shoppers' paradise, now leads on to the ★ **Campo de'Fiori**, where a market is held every weekday. At the centre of the square is a monument (1887) to Giordano Bruno, who was burnt at the stake here as a heretic in 1600.

Campo de'Fiori

Southwestwards, in the direction of the Tiber, three narrow streets lead away to the ★ **Piazza Farnese**, with its two magnificent fountains and the Renaissance **Palazzo Farnese ❼**, begun in 1514, all of it forming a very famous Roman view. The Farnese family were among the most powerful in the city in the 16th century; they appointed cardinals and even a Pope (Paul III), and their family palazzo is of exemplary magnificence. It was built by architects Sangallo, Michelangelo and Della Porta, and the numerous frescoes are by Annibale Carracci. The quiet and clearly-defined rows of windows lend the building its special magnificence; the interior courtyard with its arcades is one of the finest in Rome. The famous Galleria Carracci is now the reception room of the French embassy. At the rear of the palace there is a view down the ★ **Via Giulia**. This 16th-century street, utterly straight, has successfully retained its architectural unity. The Romans celebrate 'their' Via Giulia in May each year with courtyard concerts and illuminations.

Fountain detail, Via Guilia

Heading back in the direction of the Piazza Farnese, cross the Campo de'Fiori to reach the **Palazzo della Cancelleria ❽**, the first of the great Roman Renaissance palazzi, built between 1483 and 1511. The three-storeyed facade is particularly impressive for its windows. The right portal leads into the former palace chapel of San Lorenzo in Damaso, built by Bramante and extensively restored during the 19th century; the left portal leads to the magnificent inner courtyard, with its double loggias. The great hall is said to have been decorated in just 100 days by Giorgio Vasari with scenes from the life of Pope Paul III (1534–49); hence its name, Salone dei Cento Giorni.

A rewarding little detour along the Corso Vittorio Emanuele in the direction of the Tiber provides a fine view of the adjacent facades of the **Chiesa Nuova** and the Oratorio dei Filippini. The facade of this church, which was originally called Santa Maria in Valicella, was finished in 1605. One of Rome's patron saints, St Philip Neri (died 1595), lies buried here (left of the choir), and the apse contains three fine works by Rubens, who lived in Rome from 1606–8. The ★ **Oratorio dei Filippini** was built between 1637 and 1662 by Borromini as a place of worship for the fraternity of St Philip Neri, who instituted the musical gatherings that later became known as oratorios. The concave architectural elements are typical of Borromini's style.

Church facade, Piazza Navona

Fontana del Nettuno

20

Behind the Chiesa Nuova to the right, the Via del Governo Vecchio leads to the ★★ **Piazza Navona** ❾, where further works by Borromini can be admired. This splendid square, which occupies the site of the Circus of Domitian (65m/213ft x 240m/780ft), was laid out at the end of the 16th century. The three fountains and the striking-looking church of Sant'Agnese set against the baroque unity of the whole make the Piazza Navona one of the greatest sights in Europe. From the 17th until the mid-19th century the square was flooded every weekend for the

entertainment of the Romans, and it still retains its former festive character even today, being one of the most animated squares in Rome. The three fountains were planned in 1575; the basin was designed by Della Porta, and the statues were added later (between the 17th and 19th centuries). The southern fountain (Fontana del Moro) shows a Moor wrestling with a dolphin; the northern one (Fontana del Nettuno, 1878) represents Neptune struggling with a sea-monster; and the central fountain, the famous ★★ **Fontana dei Quattro Fiumi** (Fountain of the Four Rivers), was created by Bernini in 1651. Here he uses colossal allegorical figures to represent the rivers Ganges, Danube, Nile and Plate. The obelisk was cut in Egypt during Domitian's time (1st century). The fact that the figures on the fountains are pointing away from the church has been traced to Bernini's dislike of Borromini's facade!

The domed church of **Sant'Agnese** was begun in 1652 by Rainaldi, before Borromini took over and made the church his own. The dynamic interplay of dome, towers and facade is typical of Borromini's baroque style. This same momentum is continued in the interior, with its intricate Greek-cross ground-plan, where free-standing columns and altar sculptures create some brilliant spatial effects. Above the entrance is the monument to Pope Innocent X (buried here) who commissioned both the church and the Bernini fountain.

21

Directly opposite Sant'Agnese, a passageway links the Piazza Navona with the Corso del Rinascimento; the next side-street on the left, the Via del Salvatore, leads to the Piazza San Luigi dei Francesi with the church of the same name. **San Luigi dei Francesi** ❿ was consecrated in 1589 as the national church of the French. The two-storey Renaissance facade by Giacomo Della Porta, with its three portals, fronts a three-aisled interior; the right-hand aisle contains frescoes by Domenichino (dating from 1616–17) in the second chapel along, and the fifth chapel in the left-hand aisle has three very good ★★ **paintings** by Caravaggio: *The Calling of St Matthew, The Martyrdom of St Matthew,* and *St Matthew and the Angel.*

Shrine opposite San Luigi dei Francesci

Opposite the church, the Via Giustiniani leads to the Piazza della Rotonda and on to the ★★★ **Pantheon** ⓫, one of the best-preserved monuments of antiquity. Founded in 17BC as a pantheon to all the gods, it received its present-day appearance under Hadrian (AD117–138); as the Christian church of Santa Maria ad Martyres (from 609 onwards) it was probably the origin of the festival of All Saints (1 November).

The really fascinating aspect of this building is the way it combines the Greek pronaos with the Roman domed rotunda: the triangular gable of the portico is supported by 16 huge Corinthian columns. This model inspired not only

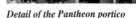

Detail of the Pantheon portico

The Oculus in the dome

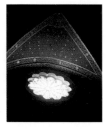

Interior detail, Santa Maria sopra Minerva

Renaissance but also neoclassical architects. The *cella*, or main body of the temple, has a **dome** that is saucer-shaped outside and a perfect hemisphere inside. The height and diameter of the interior are the same (43.4m/142ft), giving the building perfect symmetry. The seven great niches were consecrated to the seven gods of the planets; the entrance to the building is as it were the eighth niche. The interior, though architecturally stunning, is of little importance artistically; prominent among the various tombs here are those of Italian kings Victor Emmanuel II and Umberto I. Looking very modest in contrast to their magnificence is the tomb of Raphael (after the second niche to the left of the entrance) with the Madonna statue that he designed himself and which was completed by a pupil. The bronze portals are of antique origin.

To the left of the Pantheon is the **Piazza della Minerva**, containing the smallest obelisk in Rome, supported by an elephant – a delightful work by Bernini. The church of **Santa Maria sopra Minerva** ⑫ (on the site of a temple to Minerva) has a severe-looking Renaissance facade dating from 1453; its interior, however, is one of the few examples of the Gothic style in Rome (*see page 84*). The building was begun around 1280 by the Dominicans, who also built Santa Maria Novella in Florence and thus introduced the Gothic style to Rome. To finance the work, rich families were promised funerary chapels, and the church thus received some fine artistic decoration. The three-aisled interior with its crossbeam vault was rather badly restored and painted during the 19th century (1848–55). The *Cappella Caraffa* in the right transept contains some magnificent ★★ **frescoes** (1488–92) by Filippino Lippi; to the left of the main altar with its sarcophagus of St Catherine of Siena (Italy's patron saint, died 1380) is a ★ *Christ bearing the Cross* by Michelangelo; the bronze drapery is a later addition. The chapel next to the sacristy entrance in the left transept contains a fine Roman sarcophagus depicting Hercules's struggle with the lion; and the first chapel to the left of the choir contains the tomb of the famous Dominican painter-monk, Fra Beato Angelico (died 1455).

Here we leave the church. The section of street named after the painter opens out into the Via di Sant'Ignazio which leads off to the left, to the ★ **Piazza Sant'Ignazio**; the five 18th-century rococo palaces here are like a theatrical backdrop. **Sant'Ignazio** ⑬ was built between 1627 and 1685, designed by the Jesuit Orazio Grassi and consecrated to the founder of the Order, St Ignatius Loyola. The volutes on the two-storey facade give the building its unmistakably baroque look. The elaborate decoration of the interior is reminiscent of the church of Il Gesù (*see page 18*) and contrasts sharply with the medieval Gothic

Piazza Sant'Ignazio

severity of Santa Maria sopra Minerva (*see above*). The
★ **ceiling frescoes**, with their masterly use of *trompe l' oeil*
perspective, are by Andrea del Pozzo. The best view of
the ceiling is from a small yellow disc in the pavement,
roughly at the centre of the nave.

From the piazza in front of the church, the Via de'Burrò
leads to the Piazza di Pietra, where the remains of the
Temple of Hadrian have been incorporated into the facade
of the Borsa; 11 Corinthian columns can still be seen.
The Via dei Bergamaschi now leads into the ★ **Piazza
Colonna ⓮**, one of the main squares in Rome, not least
because of all the administrative buildings here: the
Palazzo Chigi (17th-century) on the northern side of the
piazza is the official residence of the Prime Minister, and
the Palazzo Montecitorio next door to it (begun by Bernini
in 1650, completed by Fontana in 1694) houses the Italian
Parliament (Chamber of Deputies). The obelisk standing
in the Piazza di Montecitorio was brought back to Rome
from Egypt by Augustus, who used it as a sundial; ar-
chaeologists are still trying to ascertain the exact function of this former temple area. The ★★ **Column of
Marcus Aurelius** at the top of the square used to stand
at the centre of another antique forum on the *Campus
Martius*. It dates from the year 180, and the bas-relief
around the shaft depicts the campaigns of Marcus Aurelius
against the Germanic tribes and the Sarmatians. As with
Trajan's Column (*see page 25*), there is a staircase inside
the column leading up to the top. The statue of the emperor
was replaced with a statue of the Apostle Paul in 1589.

The pedestrian subway beneath the Corso leads into the
Galleria Colonna, a modern, Y-shaped shopping centre.
Beyond it is the Via Santa Maria in Via, which continues as the Via del Tritone and leads on to the ★ **Piazza San
Silvestro**, with its bus station and central post office. A
short detour away, up the Via della Mercede, are two magnificent angels by Bernini in the church of Sant'Andrea
delle Fratte. Its tower is crowned by yet another unusual
idea of Borromini's. From the Piazza San Silvestro, and
the church of the same name, a shopping arcade leads to
the **Corso**, Rome's main shopping street. To the north is
the Piazza San Lorenzo in Lucina, with a turn-off leading to the church of San Lorenzo in Lucina. There was a
sacred building on this site as long ago as the 5th century; the Romanesque campanile and portico date from
the 12th century, and the church's present interior from
1650. A portion of the gridiron on which St Lawrence was
martyred is kept here.

Back on the Corso, the Via Condotti – the centre of
Rome's most elegant shopping area – now branches off
the Largo Goldoni; the historic **Caffè Greco** can also be
found here. The **Via Condotti** has one of the most famous

23

*St Paul on top of the
Marcus Aurelius column*

The Spanish Steps

Detail, artists' quarter

sights in Rome, the ★★ **Spanish Steps** (Scalinata della Trinità dei Monti) **⓯** and the square in front of them, the ★ **Piazza di Spagna**, named after the nearby Spanish Embassy to the Vatican (since 1647). John Keats died in a house here in 1821, and it is now a Keats-Shelley museum. In the right-hand (southern) corner, where the Via Due Macelli begins, lies the Palazzo di Propaganda Fide, founded for the training of missionaries, with a façade by Borromini. Another fine example of 17th-century architecture is the Palazzo di Spagna, with the column commemorating the establishment of the dogma of the Immaculate Conception (1857) in front of it. In front of the steps is the picturesque ★ **Fontana della Barcaccia**, a fountain depicting a leaking boat, by Bernini's father Pietro (1627–9). Eighteenth-century palazzi on the northern side of the square complete the harmonious architectural unity of the Piazza di Spagna.

The late baroque Spanish Steps (by Francesco de Sanctis, built between 1723–6) combine with the twin towers of the church of Santa Trinità dei Monti to form a very distinctive Roman scene. The church, attached to the French Convent of the Minims, was built between 1495 and 1585, and restored in 1816; its double staircase completes the scene. The obelisk here formerly stood in the Gardens of Sallust, and was brought to Rome in the 2nd century AD. The area between the Pincio and Piazza di Spagna is generally regarded as an **artists' quarter**; the Via del Babuino and the street parallel to it, the Via Margutta, contain many studios and galleries.

Route 2

★ Piazza Venezia – ★★ Trajan's Column – ★★ Fori Imperiali – ★★★ Forum Romanum – ★ Palatine – ★★★ Colosseum

On the eastern side of the ★ **Piazza Venezia**, opposite the Victor Emmanuel Monument, two domed churches can be seen on the right: the church of **Santa Maria di Loreto** , built in 1507, and the church of **Santissimo Nome di Maria** ⓲, built in 1738. They were both erected to commemorate the liberation of Vienna from Turkish occupation in the year 1683. One now has to imagine the Temple of Trajan standing between the two of them, with the famous ★★ **Trajan's Column** (Colonna Traiana) ⓲ standing in front of it; the column has survived intact to this day. Trajan ruled the Roman Empire from AD98–117, the first 'provincial' to do so (he came from Spain), and it was during his reign that the Empire achieved its maximum expansion (*see page 10*). Trajan conquered Dacia (modern-day Romania) in 113, and the Romanian language today derives from the Latin spoken by the Romans at that time.

The base of Trajan's Column

25

   Trajan's Column, erected in memory of his victory over the Dacians, used to be crowned by a huge statue of the emperor. The golden urn containing his ashes was placed in a vault below the column. The column consists of 18 marble drums 3½m (12ft) in diameter; a spiral frieze of bas-reliefs, 270m (885ft) in length, winds its way up the outside of the shaft. It contains around 2,700 figures measuring up to 70 cm (2ft) in size. Various phases of the Dacian campaigns (AD101–103 and 107–108) are depicted, and the effect of the whole is a great deal more impressive than the more static depictions of battle scenes on triumphal arches. Trajan's Column was a model for later imitations (Column of Marcus Aurelius, *see page 23*). Still virtually intact, and one of the finest sights in the city, it is generally considered to be the model of Roman sculptural art.

   Further eastwards, the steps of the Via Magnanapoli lead to the Via Quattro Novembre and the Largo Magnanapoli, with the entrance to the ★ **Trajan's Markets** (Foro di Traiano) ⓲. This semicircular, multi-storeyed agglomeration of buildings, built on the slopes of the Quirinale, was built before the Forum of Trajan at the beginning of the 2nd century AD. Standing in front of the semicircle on the lowest level it is worth just imagining the pillared halls of the forum proper (118m/340ft by 89m/290ft), which was originally

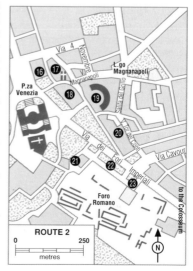

ROUTE 2
0   250
metres

Temple to Ceasar, Foro di Cesare

flanked by two colonnades. The Basilica Ulpia, with its nave and four aisles, used to stand between the forum and the column.

Leave the area via the entrance, keep to the right down the Via Quattro Novembre and turn down the next side-street, the Salità del Grillo, passing the 13th-century Torre delle Milizie, the largest fortified family tower in the city. The street continues downhill and becomes the Via di Tor de'Conti, which then leads into the Via Cavour.

Going back up the Via dei Fori Imperiali, the **Forum of Augustus** ❷⓪ can be seen on the right; here, amidst the remains of some columns on a small rise, the outlines of the ancient temple of Mars Ultor, built for Drusus and Germanicus, can still be made out.

Opposite, on the other side of the street, is the **Foro di Cesare (Caesar's Forum)** ❷①, where three Corinthian columns still stand; they once formed part of the temple of Venus Genetrix.

Continue in the direction of the Colosseum and you will pass the remains of the **Forum of Nerva** ❷② and of the **Forum of Vespasian** ❷③; much probably still remains to be excavated beneath the Via dei Fori Imperiali, laid out by Mussolini.

Roughly level with the junction with the Via Cavour is the entrance to the ★★★ **Forum Romanum** (Roman Forum). Originally a marshy valley, this area (480m/525yds in length and around 180m/195yds wide) developed into the religious, political and commercial centre of Rome; the Empire's steady expansion overstretched its resources, however, and the Imperial Fora (*see above*) had to come to the rescue. In medieval times the Forum was a heap of overgrown ruins, and as the Campo Vaccino it was also used for grazing cattle. Systematic archaeological excavation began only in 1803.

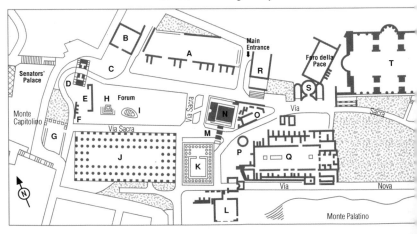

A tour of the Forum

The Via Sacra, the oldest street in Rome, runs right round the Forum and can be joined at the entrance. Walking westwards in the direction of the Capitoline, the **Basilica Aemilia** [A], an assembly hall for politicians, businessmen and moneylenders dating from the 2nd century BC, is on the right. The **Curia Senatus** [B], built under Diocletian (c 300BC), is where the Senate used to meet to control the destiny of the Empire; as a place of assembly the site dates back to the time of the city's legendary kings. The oldest monument in the Forum is the **Lapis Niger** [C], a pavement of black marble laid to mark a sacred spot; according to legend, Romulus, one of the city's founders, lies buried here. Some steps lead to a square stele with inscriptions in Latin, the oldest extant example of the language.

The Curia

The triple **Arch of Septimius Severus** (Arco di Settimio Severo) [D], built in the year 203, bears four reliefs depicting scenes from the two Persian campaigns. The **Imperial Rostrum** [E] was the orator's stage during political discussions. Behind it to the right is a cylindrical construction, the Umbilicus Urbis, which is supposed to mark the centre of the city; the Milliarium Aureum [F], or 'Golden Milestone' (a bronze-covered column set up by Augustus, showing the distances to all the chief cities of the Empire), used to stand to the left of the stage.

Arch of Septimius Severus

The eight Ionic columns in the furthermost corner of the Forum are all that remains of the **Temple of Saturn** (Tempio di Saturno) [G], founded in 498BC, which was used as the state treasury. Along the Via Sacra in the opposite direction from the Capitoline is the youngest monument in the Forum, the Corinthian **Column of Phocas** (Colonne di Foca) [H], which dates from the year 608. It was set up by Saturn, god-king of Italy, in honour of the centurion Phocas who had seized the throne of Byzantium. To the east of the column, the **Lacus Curtius** [I] must have been part of the former marsh here. It was considered sacred by the ancient Romans, and human sacrifices were thrown into its waters; according to one legend, a patriotic youth named Curtius threw himself into the small lake along with his

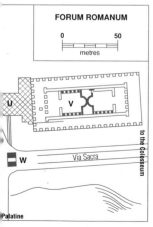

FORUM ROMANUM

0   50

metres

U

V

W   Via Sacra

to the Colosseum

Palatine

horse in 362 in order to prove that courage was the greatest Roman virtue. This is the part of the Forum where the townspeople used to assemble.

On the other side of the Via Sacra, in 50BC, Caesar built the **Basilica Julia** (Basilica Giulia) [J], originally the largest building in the Forum (101m/330ft long and 49m/160ft wide). All that remains of this two-storeyed, marble-faced structure are its pillared foundations. Opposite it, in the direction of the Colosseum, the ★★ **Temple of Castor and Pollux** [K], also known as the Temple of the Dioscuri, was built in 448BC after the victory over the Etruscans. The three Corinthian columns that remain date from the time of Augustus. Beyond them is a small marble altar with reliefs of the Heavenly Twins Castor and Pollux, as well as their sister Helena, and of their parents Jupiter and Leda. The Lacus Juturnae – its site is marked by a square marble basin – was one of the most ancient springs in the city, with healing waters.

The tour now continues southwards in the direction of the Palatine. Here, in AD365, the oldest Christian structure in the Forum was built on the site of a temple to Augustus: the church of **Santa Maria Antiqua** [L]. Its 6th-century frescoes provide valuable evidence of Early Christian art from the troubled period of the Iconoclastic Controversy. A path leads away from the church entrance, past the Temple of Castor and Pollux [K], to the foundations of the **Arch of Augustus** [M], erected in 31BC after the victory over Antony and Cleopatra at Actium. Its neighbouring structure was built just two years later: the **Temple of Julius Caesar** [N]. It occupies the site where Caesar's corpse was cremated in 44BC. Next to it are the remains of the **Regia** [O], the traditional palace of Numa Pompilius, Rome's second king, and the official headquarters of the Pontifex Maximus, the most senior of the city's high priests. The Pope still bears this title as head of the Roman Catholic Church. Directly opposite, 20 Corinthian columns surround the remains of the circular **Temple of Vesta** [P], where the six Vestals, or virgin priestesses of Vesta (goddess of the hearth), used to guard the sacred fire. The Vestal Virgins had to be from patrician families, and from a young age they had to spend 30 years of their life in the **Atrium Vestae** [Q], where they enjoyed special privileges. If a Vestal broke her vow of chastity she was buried alive. Another of her duties, apart from keeping the sacred flame, was to guard the statue of Pallas Athena, supposedly brought from Troy by Aeneas.

Near the main entrance to the Forum a broad flight of steps now leads away from the Via Sacra up to the **Temple of Antoninus and Faustina** [R], built in 141, the pronaos of which still survives. The entire complex was converted into the church of San Lorenzo in Miranda in

From the temple of the Vestal Virgins

the 12th century. The Via Sacra now slopes uphill, past an ancient cemetery (finds here date back to the Iron Age), to the **Temple of Romulus** [S], a circular structure dating from 309, which in the 6th century was integrated into the church of Santi Cosma e Damiano as its apse. The altar and triumphal arch are decorated with early 6th-century mosaics. The next prestigious building on the Via Sacra dates from imperial times: the **Basilica of Constantine and Maxentius** [T], a three-aisled basilica (surface area: 6,000sq m/7,170sq yds) that was begun by Maxentius (306–310) and completed by his successor Constantine. The 36-m (118-ft) high groin-vaulted nave used to contain a colossal statue of Constantine, the remains of which are on display in the courtyard of the Capitoline Museum. Though the roof over the nave collapsed, the aisles survived.

Fragment from the Forum

The Romanesque campanile of ★ **Santa Francesca Romana** [U], with its colourful brickwork, now catches the eye. The present building is 13th-century, though the facade was added later, in 1615. Francesca Romana (died 1440) is the patron saint of motorists, and on her festival (9 March) the street here is congested with cars. The church's former monastery buildings contain the Antiquarium of the Roman Forum (Antiquario Forense), where archaeological finds from the Forum are on display. Beyond the church, all that remains of the **Temple of Venus and Rome** [V], consecrated by Hadrian in AD136, is the section of it that used to face the Forum. Measuring 110m (360ft) by 53m (170ft), this used to be the largest temple in the city. Marking the end of the Via Sacra is the **Arch of Titus** [W]. This is the oldest triumphal arch in Rome,

29

Arch of Titus

Farnese Gardens

and was erected by Domitian in honour of his father Vespasian's capture of Jerusalem in AD70; the relief scenes portray his brother Titus's campaigns and also his divine ascent into heaven. The fine sculpture and use of spatial effect here make these reliefs masterpieces of Roman art.

A path now leads away from the Arch of Titus to the right in the direction of the Palatine. On the right here, paths and steps lead up to the Farnese Gardens (Orti Farnesiani), with their grotto of nymphs, fountain, pavilions and villa. They end at a **viewing terrace** [A] (*see map below*) with a panorama of the entire Forum.

★ *The Palatine (Palatino)*

The **Farnese Gardens**, laid out in the 16th century, are situated just above the Palace of Tiberius; the Palatine, the oldest part of the city, is a four-sided plateau where many imperial palaces were built. A subterranean vaulted passageway, the **Cryptoporticus** [B], leads to the **House of Livia** [C], which was once part of the Palace of Augustus; the rooms surrounding the atrium contain several superb ★ wall-paintings and also floor mosaics. The area of ex-

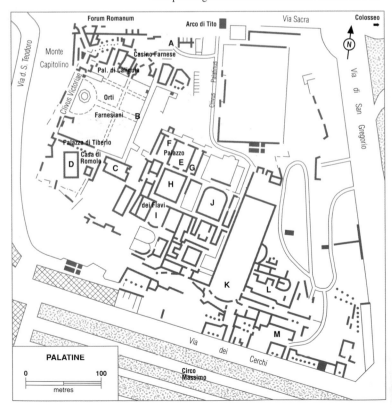

Palace of Septimius Severus

cavations right next to this building has produced the oldest finds in the city. The **Temple of Cybele** [D], built in 204BC, was consecrated to the oriental cult of the *Magna Mater*. A stairway leads to the oldest traces of settlement in Rome (8th century BC). Legend has it that Romulus's *Roma Quadrata* stood on this site – an easily defended position from which the river could have been crossed without difficulty.

31

Now come the remains of the imperial palaces proper, which lie at the centre of the Palatine. The **Domus Flavia** (House of Flavia) was built by the architect Rabirius, who received the commission from Domitian at the end of the 1st century AD. The building did full justice to the contemporary fondness for prestige and contained **reception rooms** *(Aula Regia)* [E], a three-aisled **basilica** [F], and the emperor's private **chapel** *(Larario)* [G] situated behind a **peristyle** *(Peristilio)* [H] and the **banqueting hall** *(Triclinio)* [I].

Domus Flavian

Further south is the **Domus Augustana** [J], which was built at the end of the 1st century AD, and was the private residence of the emperor. A little further southwards is the **Stadium** (Stadio Domiziano) [K], the vast outline of which (160m/525ft long, 47m/154ft wide) can still clearly be recognised. Legend has it that St Sebastian was martyred here.

And finally we arrive at the huge and impressive ruins of the **Palace and Baths of Septimius Severus** [L]. From the **Belvedere viewing platform** [M] there is a fine panorama of the Aventine and of the Circus Maximus lying in between.

To leave the Palatine, go back to the entrance and to the Arch of Titus; from there, the ★★★ **Colosseum** is just a few steps away (bus, Metro; *see page 52*).

Santa Maria d'Aracoeli, detail of the funeral of St Bernard

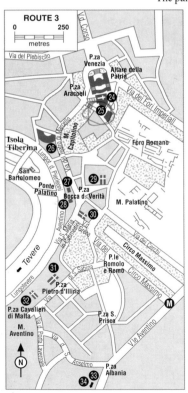

Route 3

★ Piazza Venezia – ★★ Santa Maria d'Aracoeli – ★ Capitoline Hill – ★ Theatre of Marcellus – ★ Bocca della Verità – Aventine Hill – Porta San Paolo – ★★ San Paolo fuori le Mura

Of the two stairways leading from the **★ Piazza Venezia** up the Capitoline Hill – the smallest of Rome's seven hills – the one on the left is the older: its 124 steps were built in the year 1348, and it is familiarly referred to as the 'ladder to heaven' for newly-weds. It comes to an end in front of the bare brick facade of the church of **★★ Santa Maria d'Aracoeli ㉔**. This site was previously occupied by the Temple of Juno Moneta, which contained the Roman mint (the English word 'money' and the French *monnaie* are both derived from it), and it was here that the Emperor Augustus was informed of Christ's birth. The present church was built by Franciscans in around 1250; the 22 antique columns dividing the three-aisled interior and the bright light inside the basilica make it appear almost cheerful. The paintings on the ceiling commemorate the naval victory over the Turks at Lepanto in 1571. There are many other magnificent paintings and sculptures here, and also a fine domed chapel in the left transept, with the *ara coeli*, the Altar of Heaven commissioned by Augustus, set into the pavement. The first side-chapel to the right contains some very graceful **★ frescoes** (1485), by the Umbrian painter Bernardino Pinturicchio, depicting St Bernard of Siena.

Steps lead down from the exit in the right transept to the level of the Piazza del Campidoglio **㉕** (also known as the **Capitoline Square**); the Via San Pietro in Carcere carries on downwards and turns into a staircase, with the 16th-century church of San Giuseppe dei Falegnami at its foot. Beneath it is the **★ Carcere Mamertino** (Mamertine Prison). This former Roman state prison, which dates from the 4th century BC, is thought to have once housed the Apostles Peter and Paul, who converted and baptised their fellow inmates. In the 16th century the area became the chapel of San Pietro in Carcere (St Peter Imprisoned).

If we now go back via the street and the steps we come to the rear side of the magnificent **★★ Piazza del Campidoglio ㉕**, which was designed by Michelangelo. The Renaissance architecture in this square retains its superb unity even without the equestrian statue of Marcus

Aurelius at its centre, which has now been placed in the Capitoline Museum. The balustrade on which Michelangelo placed his colossal sculptures of Castor and Pollux successfully enhances the view of the three stately palaces surrounding the square; the trapezoid ground-plan avoids any right-angles, and the fine pavement with its oval star design adds to the grandeur of the whole. The Palazzo dei Conservatori and the ★ **Capitoline Museum** stand opposite one another and are architecturally similiar: Ionic columns support a flat open loggia below, and there are magnificent rows of windows with coupled columns; Corinthian pilasters unite the two storeys. Michelangelo gave the Palazzo Senatorio – which is built on the site of the antique *Tabularium* (state archive) – a double staircase, thus providing the whole square with a perspective focal point. The triangular area formed by the two ramps contains a fountain with a statue of the *Dea Roma* (formerly a statue of Minerva); she is flanked by statues of the Nile (left, with the Sphinx) and the Tiber (right, with the she-wolf).

Researching the route

All three palaces are surrounded by a balustrade adorned with statues, which is exceptionally picturesque when illuminated by oil-lamps on the evening of 21 April, Rome's legendary birthday (753BC). Above the Palazzo Senatorio is a campanile (1580) crowned by a statue of Minerva and a gilded cross. The Palazzo Senatorio is the official seat of the Mayor of Rome; the other two buildings are now museums. The famous Treaty of Rome, which established the EC, was signed in the main hall of the Palazzo dei Conservatori in 1957.

33

Palazzo Senatorio

The head and other fragments of Emperor Constantine

The Capitoline Museums

(Opening hours: Tuesday to Saturday 9am–2pm; Sunday 9am–1pm; Tuesday and Saturday also open 5–8pm; closed Monday).

Palazzo dei Conservatori. The fragments of a colossal statue of Emperor Constantine the Great in the inner courtyard are particularly interesting; the statue formerly stood in the Basilica of Constantine (*see page 29*), and the foot and the head give an idea of its sheer size (around 12m/40ft high). The famous ★★ **She-Wolf** of Rome (in the Sala della Lupa, first floor) can be seen suckling the city's legendary founders, Romulus and Remus; dated at around 500BC, this bronze statue is thought to be of Etruscan origin, and the twins were added later by the Florentine artist Antonio Pollaiuolo (16th-century).

The halls on the first floor document several episodes of Roman history. The Sala degli Orazi e Curiazi contains a marble statue of Pope Urban VIII (1623–44) by Bernini and also a bronze statue of his successor, Innocent X (1644–55) by Algardi; both statues are distinctively Roman baroque. In the Sala delle Oche, next door to the Sala della Lupa, there is a bronze bust of Michelangelo, and also a mastiff in rare green marble. The highlight of the Galleria degli Orti Lamiani is the Esquiline Venus, a very graceful work of the school of Pasiteles (1st-century BC). The ★ **Pinacoteca Capitolina** (Capitoline Picture Gallery) contains several important 16th to 18th-century works by artists such as Bellini, Titian, Tintoretto, Caravaggio and Van Dyck.

'Fortune-teller' by Caravaggio

The Palazzo Caffarelli, on the right behind the Palazzo dei Conservatori, was once the Prussian Embassy. Since 1925 it has housed the Museo Nuovo, containing finds dating from the Republic and the remains of the Temple of Jupiter that once stood on the Capitoline.

★ **Capitoline Museum** (Museo Capitolino). Among the many exhibits here, don't miss the following: the ★ **equestrian statue of Marcus Aurelius**; the Sala del Gladiatore on the 1st floor; and the ★ **statue** of the *Dying Gaul*, a Roman copy of an original of the Pergamon school (2nd-century). The Sala degli Imperatori contains 64 portraits of Roman emperors; next door, in the Sala dei Filosofi, is Rome's most extensive collection of portraits, with poets, philosophers and statesmen, and also – in the central hall – a 5th-century Greek bronze of a *Wounded Amazon*. The Gabinetto della Venere, a small room off the main corridor, contains the ★ **Capitoline Venus**, a Roman replica of a Hellenistic original in Parian marble, which Goethe considered the finest antique statue in Rome. On the ground floor, in Hall 1 (Culti Orientali), there are three fine representations of Mithras.

The Dying Gaul

From the Piazza del Campidoglio, the Cordonata, Michelangelo's Renaissance staircase, leads past the unassuming 19th-century statue of Cola di Rienzo, marking the spot where he was killed in 1354, and down on to the Via del Teatro di Marcello. This stepped ramp is also illuminated on Rome's birthday, and its Renaissance splendour contrasts nicely with the medieval Aracoeli church and stairway. Michelangelo placed two Egyptian lions in black granite at the foot of the steps.

Walking towards the Tiber now, we approach the oldest part of the city; on the right-hand side of the street are the ruins of the ★ **Theatre of Marcellus ㉖** , commissioned by Augustus in 13BC, and with a seating capacity of 15,000. The Forum Boarium (Rome's cattle market) used to stand of the site of today's ★ **Piazza Bocca della Verità**, and excavations on the slopes of the Palatine facing the Tiber (Area Sacra di Sant'Omobono) have revealed traces of human habitation dating back to the 9th century BC. The **Temple of Portunus ㉗** (formerly called the Temple of Fortuna Virilis) was built in around 100BC. Its lack of monumental grandeur reveals that it belongs to the transitional style of architecture under the Republic. The small round **Temple of Hercules Victor ㉘** next to it, often wrongly referred to as the Temple of Vesta because of its similarity to the one in the Forum (*see page 28*), was built in the Greek style during the reign of Augustus and its original function remains unclear; during the Middle Ages it was consecrated to St Stephen.

Opposite, the Via del Velabro leads to the Arch of Janus, which used to form a covered passage at a crossroads and was probably built in the 4th century AD, and beyond it is the Roman basilica of ★ **San Giorgio in Velabro ㉙**. In July 1993, this building, which dates from the 7th century, was badly damaged by a bomb. The 12th-century porch was completely destroyed, but the bell-tower, also dating from the 12th century, remained unharmed. Inside are antique columns, an altar tabernacle and 7th-century frescoes. To the left of the church is the small Arcus Argentariorum, built by the city's money-changers and cattle-dealers in honour of Septimius Severus. When the region was still marshland, this is where – according to legend – the shepherd Faustulus first discovered the basket containing Romulus and Remus, the city's founders.

Another Romanesque jewel is the basilica of **Santa Maria in Cosmedin ㉚** . Built with just one aisle in the 6th century, it was given a further two in the 8th century. The ★ **campanile**, one of the finest in Rome, dates from the 12th century, as does the portico. The marble face set into the wall beneath it is known as the ★ **Bocca della Verità**; according to legend its mouth would close upon the hand of any liar who placed it there. It is in fact an

35

Temple of Hercules Victor

Basilica Santa Sabina

Ceremonial gathering,
Porta San Paolo

ancient drain cover. The ★ **interior** of the basilica contains 18 antique columns, and there is some fine Cosmati decoration (*see page 50*) on the choir screens, rood-loft and episcopal throne. The ★ **mosaic pavement** is 12th-century, and the Gothic baldachin above the high altar dates from 1294. Cardinal Alfano (early 12th-century) wanted to immortalise himself via the interior decoration of this church; he lies buried to the right of the portal.

On leaving the church, keep to the left and cross the Via della Greca; the next turn-off to the left leads up to the **Aventine Hill** (Monte Aventino); on the Via di Santa Sabina is the 5th-century basilica of ★ **Santa Sabina** ㉛. Various later additions (choir-screens, 9th-century altar) have done little to change the original appearance of this Early Christian church. There is a remarkable 5th-century wooden ★★ **door** in the portico, with 18 panels carved with scriptural scenes. The three-aisled interior is divided by 24 Corinthian columns of Parian marble; the warm light shining through the yellowish selenite windows gives Santa Sabina its special atmosphere. The original, profane function of the basilica as a legal and commercial centre can still be sensed here. On the inner wall of the entrance there are some 5th-century mosaics, some of the oldest in Rome, showing the founder's name and also two female figures representing the Church of the Jews and the Church of the Gentiles.

The restoration work on this basilica has been exemplary. The same cannot be said, however, of the next church along the Via Santa Sabina, **Sant'Alessio** ㉜. It also dates back to the Early Middle Ages, and is in the form of a three-aisled basilica. However, baroque additions in around 1750 deprived the church of the original convincing clarity. The church contains a wooden staircase that is revered as a relic: St Alexis (Sant'Alessio) lived and died beneath it. The Via Santa Sabina comes out into the Piazza dei Cavalieri di Malta, with elaborate 18th-century decoration by Piranesi. There is also a remarkable view of the dome of St Peter's through a keyhole in the doorway of the Maltese Villa.

The Aventine today is a quiet residential area; this becomes clear as you walk down the Via di Sant'Anselmo to the Piazza Albania. From there, the Viale Piramide Cestia leads to the **Porta San Paolo** ㉝. Once part of the Aurelian Wall (*see page 68*), this was the old city-gate to Ostia; the square here with the wall, the gate and the ★ **Pyramid of Gaius Cestius** is one of the most remarkable views in the city. The pyramid contains the tomb of the praetor and tribune of the plebs, Gaius Cestius, who died in 12BC. Its sheer scale (27m/88ft high) reflects imperial Rome's predilection for all things Egyptian. Two stops away from the Metro station of Piramide

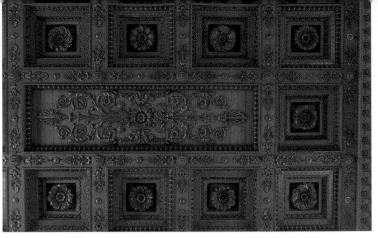

is the basilica of ★★ **San Paolo fuori le Mura** **34**, the second largest church in Rome after St Peter's. In around AD400, a small shrine above the tomb of the Apostle Paul was turned into a five-aisled basilica, the dimensions of which corresponded to those of the Basilica Ulpia in the Trajan's Markets (*see page 25*); the early Christians wanted to match the achievements of the 'pagans' before them. This was the largest church in Christendom until the new St Peter's was built in the 16th century, and it was elaborately decorated with frescoes and mosaics; in 1823, however, the entire edifice burnt down. The present building is a reconstruction, and was consecrated by Pius IX in 1854.

The coffered ceiling, San Paolo fuori le Mura

Survivals from the former building include the triumphal arch, with its restored 5th-century mosaics, the apse (13th-century mosaics), the 5-m (16-ft) high paschal candlestick (12th-century) and also the tabernacle, supported by four porphyry columns, above the Gothic high altar (1285), beneath which the Apostle's tomb lies. The luxuriant white-and-gold stucco ceiling, decorated with the arms of Pius IX, was added in place of the original open timber roof, and below the windows, running right round the interior, there is a frieze of mosaic portraits showing all the Popes, which is divided up by 80 granite columns. The north portico contains 12 antique marble columns taken from the old basilica. The right transept leads to the ★★ **cloisters** (*chiostro*): the mosaic decoration there (1205–41) is masterly. The reconstruction was given a huge colonnaded quadriporticus in front of its western facade, but this seems far too monumental nowadays, and the 19th-century neoclassical statues and mosaics tend to mar the original impact of the building as a whole.

The portico and facade

There are buses back to the city centre from the square in front of the basilica. The trip is also a good way of familiarising oneself with the layout of the city.

Baths of Caracalla

Wall fragments

Route 4

★★ Baths of Caracalla – Porta San Sebastiano – ★★ Via Appia Antica

Travel by bus from the ★ **Piazza Venezia** to the Piazzale Numa Pompilio stop; right next to it is the entrance to the ★★ **Baths of Caracalla** *(*Terme di Caracalla*)* **35** (open daily 9am–dusk, Sunday 9am–1pm). These mighty imperial *thermae*, now a skeleton, once stood in a park used for sports, around which were grouped halls for lectures and plays. Septimius Severus began the construction of these massive public baths in 206, and his son Caracalla opened them in 216. The complex as a whole was 330m (1082ft) in length, and the main building was 220m/720ft by 14m (46ft); it could accommodate up to 1,500 guests at any one time. The baths were in use right up to the Gothic invasion in the 6th century, and were famed for their magnificence, manifest not only in inlaid floors, glass mosaics, alabaster and marble columns and Greek sculptures, but also in a Latin and a Greek library. Fragments of the architecture and decoration can still be admired today. Opera performances take place on the site in the summer months.

From the Piazzale Numa Pompilio, the Via Porta San Sebastiano leads to the Porta San Sebastiano city gate; here we arrive at the entrance to the **Tomb of the Scipios** (Sepolcro degli Scipioni) **36** (open daily except Monday 9am–2pm; also 4–7pm on Tuesday, Thursday and Saturday). Alongside the excavated remains of a Roman house is the tomb of the Scipios, who were one of the most important Roman families during the Republican era. The sarcophagi date from the 2nd and 3rd century BC; the niches once contained funerary urns. The nearby ★ **Columbarium of Pomponius Hylas** contains some interesting paintings dating from Augustus's time. The **Porta San Sebastiano 37** is one of the 13 city gates that made up the 19-km (12-mile) long Aurelian Wall, erected by Aurelius between 270 and 275. It houses the Museo delle Mura (open Tuesday to Saturday 9am–2.30pm; also 4–6pm on Tuesday, Thursday and Saturday).

Outside this city gate is the start of the ★★ **Appian Way**. It was laid out in the 4th century BC and used to lead via the Albanian Mountains and Capua to Brundisium (Brindisi). It was referred to by Statius as *regina viarum* (queen of roads). Today it is a series of ruins set against attractive landscape. The Romans were forbidden from the 5th century BC onwards to bury their dead within the city walls, and so the Via Appia became a street lined with tombs. Rather than walking along it and being bothered by the noisy traffic it is best to take a No 118 bus. Around

Porta San Sebastiano

Continuation in right-hand column

ROUTE 4

0   250

metres

Domine Quo Vadis

Catacombs of St Calixtus

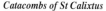

half a mile further on we pass the little church of **Domine Quo Vadis 38**, where the Apostle Peter, on fleeing from martyrdom in Rome, met Christ on the road and asked him, '*Domine Quo Vadis?*' ('Where are you going, Lord?'). Christ answered, '*Venio iterum crucifigi*' ('I have come to be crucified a second time') – whereupon Peter returned to Rome and martyrdom.

The area of the **catacombs** – the underground cemeteries of the early Christians – is around half a mile further on; the romantic notion that they were also inhabited has been refuted long since. According to Early Christian tradition, the subterranean passageways were used only for funeral repasts, and the not easily definable transition from the cult of Mithras to Christianity (*see pages 51* and *83*) also caused a lot of confusion, since the two religions had many similarities as far as ritual was concerned – though this has been categorically denied until the present day by the Church of Rome. Near Via Appia Antica 110 is the entrance to the **★★ Catacombs of St Calixtus** (Catacombe di San Callisto) **39**. Before Christianity received official recognition, the practice was to position the cemeteries around the tomb of a martyr. The Catacombs of St Calixtus were started in the 2nd century and were given their papal crypt in the 3rd century. This four-level subterranean structure with up to 20km (13 miles) of known passageways is one of the most famous cemeteries in Rome. The underground burial chambers were retained until the collapse of the Roman Empire, when destruction of the city at the hands of enemy troops caused the popes to transfer their holy relics to churches inside the city. The underground necropoli were then forgotten – until they were rediscovered in the 16th century and systematically explored in the 19th. They are decorated with frescoes and inscriptions. The papal crypt dates from the 3rd century, and the adjoining *cubiculum* used to contain the tomb of St Cecilia, which was transferred to the church of Santa Cecilia in Trastevere. The oldest part of the catacombs is the crypt of Lucina. Conducted tours are obligatory if you wish to visit the catacombs (open daily except Wednesday 8.30am–12noon and 2.30–6pm, and until 5pm in winter).

On the left-hand side of the Via Appia we now come to the **Jewish Catacombs**, the entrance to which is near No 119A, and then the road descends to a small piazza, with the **Basilica of San Sebastiano 40** on the right at No 132 (open daily 9am–12noon and 2.30–5pm). It was built in the 4th century, and in the 9th century was consecrated to St Sebastian; baroque additions in 1612 lent it its present-day appearance. The Catacombs of San Sebastiano can be reached via the church (conducted tours only; open daily except Thursday 9am–12noon and 2.30–5.30pm, and until 5pm in winter). The Via delle Sette Chiese, which joins the Via Appia just before the basilica, leads to the equally fascinating Catacombs of St Domitilla, where a guide is also compulsory (open daily except Tuesday 9am–12noon and 2.30–5.30pm, in winter until 5pm).

Antique monuments now follow along the Appian Way; the **Mausoleum of Romulus** (Tempio di Romolo) **41**, a round structure, used to stand in the middle of a vast court-yard 100-m (328-ft) square; the walls can just be made out. This Romulus was the son of Maxentius, and he died in 309. Directly beyond the mausoleum, the **Circus of Maxentius** (Circo di Massenzio) **42** can be seen. Built in the year 309, this chariot-racing stadium (482m/1580ft long and 70m/230ft wide) could accommodate around 18,000 spectators. At the centre is a small rise; an obelisk once stood here before Bernini used it to adorn the main fountain in the Piazza Navona (*see page 21*). At this stage it's certainly worth continuing along the cypress-lined Via Appia as far as the well-preserved and very majestic ★ **Tomb of Cecilia Metella** **43**. The tomb is in such good condition because it was transformed into a battlemented tower to serve as the keep of a castle in 1299. This cylindrical structure is 20m (65ft) in diameter and was built in the middle of the 1st century for the wife of Crassus, elder son of the triumvir Crassus, one of Caesar's generals in Gaul (open daily Tuesday to Saturday 9am–1.30pm, Sunday 9am–12.30pm).

A walk along the Appian Way is like a stroll through a vast archaeological park: time really does seem to stand still in this spacious, silent Mediterranean landscape, filled with the ruins of past greatness.

A No 118 bus will take you back to the hectic, everyday life of Rome's city centre.

Outside the catacombs

41

Along the Appian Way

Route 5

★ Piazza Venezia – ★★ Fontana di Trevi – ★ Palazzo del Quirinale – Via Quattro Fontane – Via Nazionale – ★ Baths of Diocletian – Stazione Termini

From the ★ **Piazza Venezia**, go a short way along the Via C Battisti and then branch off left to the **Piazza Apostoli**. The long square is dominated by the mighty facade of the **Palazzo Colonna ⓘ**, which received its present-day appearance after alteration work in 1730. The palazzo was begun by Pope Martin V (1417–31), a member of the Colonna family, and it contains the magnificent ★ **Galleria Colonna**, which displays works by Titian, Tintoretto and Veronese, but is also worth admiring for its splendid decoration. The *salone* and the adjoining halls, altogether 76m (250ft) in length, are lent further emphasis by impressive ceiling frescoes. The entrance to the Galleria is at Via della Pilotta 17, round the back of the building (open Saturday only, 9am–1pm and by appointment).

Inside the palace complex is the basilica of the **Santi Apostoli ⓘ**, which was built by Pelagius I (579–590) after the defeat and expulsion of the Goths. It underwent Renaissance and baroque alterations in the 16th and early 17th centuries respectively, and was finally given a neo-classical facade in 1827. The portico is crowned by statues of the 12 Apostles, and its right-hand inner wall contains a 2nd-century Roman bas-relief of an imperial eagle holding an oak wreath. The ceiling frescoes above the three-aisled baroque interior are by Baciccia (1707), who also painted those in the Il Gesù (*see page 18*). Opposite

Ceiling fresco, Basilica Santi Apostoli

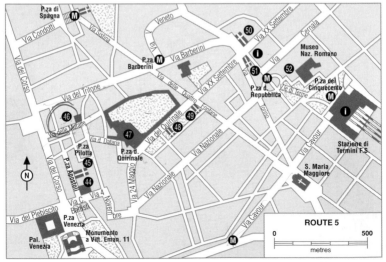

the church is a palace designed by Bernini, the Palazzo Odescalchi, which has a very fine interior courtyard.

The route now leads along the Via Vaccaro, the Piazza della Pilotta and Vicolo Monticello, across a patio with impressive paintings, as far as the Via delle Muratte and the very ornate ★★ **Fontana di Trevi** ④, the most impressive fountain in a city that has no shortage of them. The Fontana di Trevi is particularly theatrical because of the fact that it only comes into view at the very last moment from all the narrow streets leading towards it. At the rear of the fountain is a triumphal arch with four Corinthian columns supporting a frieze with statues of the Four Seasons, and with the arms of the Corsini family at the top. At the centre is the sea-god Neptune with his winged chariot being drawn by two giant tritons. The Fontana di Trevi is one of the city's most exuberant and successful 18th-century monuments. Possibly based on a design by Bernini, it was built 50 years after his death by Niccolò Salvi, between 1732 and 1751, and the Neptune was added by Pietro Bracci in 1762.

Fontana di Trevi

The Via San Vincenzo now leads uphill from the fountain, and the Via della Dataria branches off it towards the Quirinale. Some steps lead up to the ★ **Piazza del Quirinale**, which almost resembles a loggia overlooking the panorama of the city below, with the dome of St Peter's in the distance. The Quirinal (61m/200ft) is the highest of Rome's seven hills. At the centre of the piazza are colossal statues of the Dioscuri or Heavenly Twins, Castor and Pollux, Roman copies of Greek originals dating from the 5th century BC. The **Palazzo del Quirinale** ④ was begun in 1574 as a summer residence for the Popes; in 1870 the Italian kings moved in, and since 1947 it has been the official residence of the President of the Republic. The huge portal in the Renaissance facade is by Bernini, and the courtyard contains a spiral staircase with Doric double columns. In the stairwell there are fragments of frescoes from the apse of Santi Apostoli (viewing by prior arrangement). The flank of this building, which because of its length is also known as the *manica lunga* (the long sleeve), lies on the Via del Quirinale.

43

Band members outside Palazzo del Quirinale

The small church of ★ **Sant'Andrea al Quirinale** ④ opposite was built by Bernini as the chapel of a Jesuit college. It has a remarkable elliptical ground-plan, balanced by its simple facade of a single order. Sant' Andrea was built between 1658 and 1671, and magnificent interior decoration – including its gilded dome and stucco work – made it one of the finest baroque structures in Rome. Not all that surprising that Bernini's arch-rival Borromini also built a little church just down the street, ★ **San Carlo alle Quattro Fontane** ④, also known as San Carlino. Unfortunately for him, though, it was

San Carlo alle Quattro Fontane

commissioned by impoverished Spanish monks rather than wealthy Jesuits. Displaying his fondness for convex and concave surfaces yet again (Oratorio dei Filippini, Sant' Agnese, *see Route 1, page 16*), Borromini dispensed with right-angles altogether here.

The little church was begun in 1638, though it was 1663 before the monks had managed to collect enough money for the facade. Borromini also gave the church an elliptical dome, crowned by a double lantern. This San Carlo (there are three in Rome) was the first building designed purely by Borromini. The church gets its name 'Alle Quattro Fontane' from the four small fountains in niches at each corner of this busy crossroads with its four vistas, typical of the Rome of Sixtus V (1585–90).

Door handle at Santa Maria della Vittoria

The Via del Quirinale now continues as the Via XX Settembre; on the left-hand side of it, on the level of the Piazza San Bernardo, is the church of **Santa Maria della Vittoria** ❺⓿, built by Carlo Maderna in 1605 and given its two-storey baroque facade with its volutes by Soria in 1625. The fourth chapel on the left inside this ornate, single-aisled baroque church contains an important work of art: Bernini's most famous sculpture, ★★ **The Ecstasy of St Teresa**, which uses the shallow space to great effect.

Bernini's St Teresa

On the other side of the square is the Fontanone dell' Acqua Felice, a monumental fountain with a pallid figure of Moses that has never been popular since it was erected in 1587, and a little further away is the round church of **San Bernardo alle Terme** ❺❶. It dates from antiquity, and was built into one of the two circular halls flanking the exedra of the Baths of Diocletian (*see below*) in the 16th century. The Via Torino, intersected by the Via Nazionale, begins here; it is one of the main shopping streets in the city, with the interesting Palazzo dei Esposizione at its centre. It opens up to the left on to the Piazza della Repubblica, where the semicircular, porticoed facades of its buildings follow the line of the exedra of the former imperial baths. The Fountain of the Naiads here dates from 1885. It caused a scandal when it was unveiled, because of the allegedly obscene postures of the nymphs. Elegant shops once lined the square, but in recent years they have been ousted by tawdry sex cinemas.

The ★ **Baths of Diocletian** ❺❷, opened in the year 305, were modelled after the Baths of Caracalla (*see page 38*), and were even larger. They could accommodate up to 3,000 people, and covered an area measuring 356m (389yds) by 316m (345yds). During the Middle Ages they fell into disrepair, and when the original vault was converted into a Carthusian monastery in the 16th century Michelangelo was commissioned to build the monastery church, which he duly integrated into the existing architecture. The entrance to the church of **Santa Maria degli**

Angeli lies on the Piazza della Repubblica opposite the junction of the Via Nazionale, and a passageway leads into the nave; as a result of late baroque alterations (1749) of Michelangelo's plans, the transept, measuring over 90m (295ft), is now longer than the actual nave itself. The decoration is also late baroque.

Next door to this church is the **★★ Museo Nazionale Romano**, which contains one of the largest collections of antique art in Europe (Tuesday to Saturday 9am–2pm, Sunday 9am–1pm; visitors should note that many items will be transferred to the new archaeological museum opposite the Stazione Termini). Here are just a few of the most famous exhibits: *Daughter of Niobe* (5th-century BC); *Ludovisi Throne*, a fine Greek original (460BC) depicting the rising of Aphrodite from the sea; *Hermes Ludovisi*; *Juno Ludovisi*; *Discobolos of Castel Porziano*; *Venus of Cyrene* (4th-century BC Greek original); *Ephebus of Subiaco*; *Maiden of Anzio*. The museum also has the largest collection of Roman sarcophagi in the world. The **★★ Great Cloister** (Grande Chiostro), 80m (260ft) square and with 100 pillars, was designed by Michelangelo. It is populated by hundreds of ancient statues and busts.

The Piazza dei Cinquecento, situated between the Museo Nazionale and the main station (**Stazione Termini**) has a bus-station.

It is one of the biggest piazzas in the city, now used not only as a major bus teminal but also as a general meeting-place. In the background on the left in front of the station buildings is the best preserved fragment of the Servian Wall, composed of massive blocks of tufa; it was the city's first wall (*see page 9*).

Museo Nazionale Romano, exterior colonnade

45

The Great Cloister

Tour guide

Route 6

Stazione Termini – ★★★ Santa Maria Maggiore – ★★ Santa Prassede – ★★ San Giovanni in Laterano – ★★ San Clemente – Oppian Hill – ★ San Pietro in Vincoli – ★★★ Colosseum

The main station (Stazione Termini) connects the busy Via Cavour, which runs between the historic Viminal and Esquiline hills, with the area around the Roman Forum

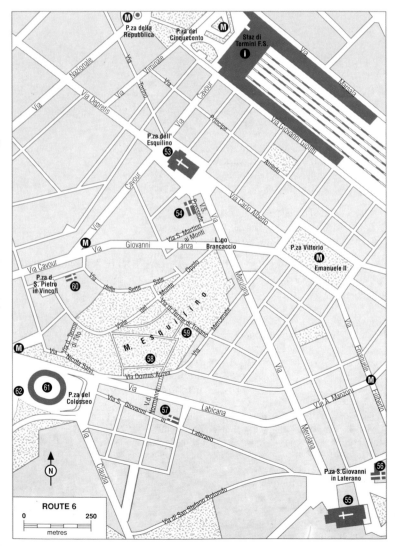

(*see page 26*). At the Piazza dell'Esquilino, the street laid out by Sixtus V (1585–90) branches off towards the Scalinata della Trinità dei Monti, or Spanish Steps (*see page 24*). The broad flight of steps on the other side of the square leads to the rear facade of ★★★ **Santa Maria Maggiore** 🛑, another of Rome's great patriarchal basilicas (*Maggiore* means great) alongside St Peter's, San Paolo fuori le Mura, and San Giovanni in Laterano. Under the 1929 concordat these churches enjoy extraterritorial privileges.

According to a 13th-century legend, the Virgin appeared to Pope Liberius and John, a patrician Roman, on the night of 4 August 352, telling them to build a church on the spot where they would find a patch of snow in the morning covering the exact area to be built over. The prediction was fulfilled, and Liberius drew up the plans. A pontifical Mass held every 5 August commemorates this miraculous fall of snow. In its present form the building dates from the 16th to 18th century, and it is entered via the profane-looking rear facade. Forming the basis of the building is a three-aisled basilica divided by 40 Ionic columns dating back to the 5th century. The ★ **Cosmati** (*see page 50*) pavement is 12th-century; the ★ **mosaic panels** on the architrave between the pillars and the windows date from 432–40; and the ★ **coffered ceiling** was gilded by the Borgia Pope Alexander VI (1492–1503) with the first gold Columbus brought from America. The mosaics over the triumphal arch are also 5th-century; those in the apse are by Jacopo Torriti (1292–95). The high altar, with its baldachin supported by four antique porphyry columns, has a statue of Pope Pius IX kneeling in prayer, dating from the last century. The Cappella delle Reliquie has 10 fine porphyry columns. In the right transept is the Cappella Sistina, built on a domed Greek-cross plan by Domenico Fontana as

Santa Maria Maggiore

The Cosmati pavement

Apse mosaic detail

Santa Prassede doorway

is the Cappella Paolina, completed for Pope Paul V in 1611 by Flaminio Ponzo. The latter contains a very popular *Madonna and Child* (13th-century). A portico with a loggia was placed in front of the main facade in 1743; at the rear of the loggia there are some early 14th-century mosaics from the facade of the previous structure on the site. The whole is crowned by the highest campanile (built in 1377) in all Rome, and the Piazza Santa Maria Maggiore in front of the church contains the only surviving column (15m/50ft high) from the Basilica of Maxentius (*see page 29*), placed there in 1614; a statue of the Virgin stands on top of it today.

The Via Santa Prassede leads away from the piazza; it contains the rather inconspicuous side-entrance to the church of ★★ **Santa Prassede ➎** . Structural changes made during later centuries have altered the original architectural clarity of this three-aisled basilica, which dates from the year 822; however, the magnificently preserved 9th-century ★★ **mosaics** are what really make this church worth visiting. The mosaics on the triumphal arch depict the New Jerusalem; those in the apse show the apotheosis of St Praxedes, sister of Pudentiana. The ★★ **Cappella di San Xenone** (Chapel of St Zeno), entered via the right transept, is the finest example of Byzantine art in Rome. This mausoleum for the mother of St Paschal has a vaulted interior entirely lined with mosaics, a work attributed to Greek artists. The crypt contains the bones of 2,000 martyrs that Pope Paschal had transferred here from the catacombs. Because of its beauty the Chapel of St Zeno used to be known as the Garden of Paradise during the Middle Ages. In a niche on the right is the stump of a column brought from Jerusalem to Rome in 1223, said to be part of the one at which Christ was scourged.

The Via Santa Prassede joins the Via San Martino ai Monti, which in turn leads off to the left to join the Via Merulana. Follow the latter in a southerly direction; it ends at the **Piazza di San Giovanni in Laterano ➏** . One can either take a leisurely stroll along the tree-lined avenue to get here, or take a bus instead. This square contains some of the most important monuments in Christian history: the basilica of St John Lateran, the Lateran Palace, the Baptistery of St John and the Scala Santa (Holy Staircase).

The Emperor Constantine presented the land here to St Melchiades (pope from 311–4) who in 314 built the five-storey basilica of ★★ **San Giovanni in Laterano** (St John Lateran). The architectural novelty here was the transept, and thus the cruciform ground-plan that differed from the antique basilica. A 'pagan' vault (such as that of the Basilica of Maxentius, built only a few years beforehand, *see page 29*) was dispensed with here. This initial building, though subjected to several architectural alterations, lasted until 1650; as the papal church and the *caput et mater omnium ecclesiarum*, the basilica was the seat of five General Councils: in 1123, 1139, 1179, 1215 and 1512. Sixtus V (1585–90) had it restored by Domenico Fontana, and in 1650 Pope Innocence X commissioned Borromini to rebuild the church yet again; the main facade with its pillared portico, loggia, attic and colossal statues was finally completed only in 1735. In July 1993, the north portal was badly damaged by a terrorist bomb; at the time of going to press, renovation work was still in progress.

Coming from the Via Merulana – and passing the tallest obelisk in Rome, originally Egyptian (15th-century BC) and 31m (100ft) high – the first part of the basilica one reaches is the ★ **Baptistery of St John** in the southwest corner of the piazza, which dates from the time of Constantine. This octagonal structure contains eight porphyry columns and a green basalt font; 2nd-century bronze doors lead into the Cappella del Battista, and the adjoining chapels contain mosaics dating from the 5th–7th century. Back in the piazza, directly opposite the Lateran Palace, the ★ **Scala Santa** ⓯, or Holy Staircase, and the Chapel of St Laurence, or Sancta Sanctorum (the private chapel of the pope), are housed in a building designed by Fontana in 1589. The 28 marble steps of the staircase, which is supposed to be the one in Pilate's house ascended by Christ after he was condemned, are protected by wooden boards and may be ascended only by worshippers on their knees. The chapel in its present version is 13th-century, and contains precious relics. The square in front of the main facade leads to the portico (containing a statue of Constantine on the left-hand side); the five doors correspond to the nave and four aisles; the **central bronze doors** came from the Curia in the Roman Forum. The Lateran Palace can be visited (via the portico) on the first Sunday in every month.

49

The central bronze doors

The interior of the **basilica** itself, which is 130m (425ft) long, corresponds to the plan of the original building: nave and four aisles, transept, and apse. Colossal statues of the Apostles were erected in the niches of the massive piers in 1718, and the **gilded wood ceiling** was completed in 1567. It had to remain unaltered when the church was rebuilt in 1650. This handicap and also the sheer scale of the church seem not to have fired Borromini's usually astounding imagination as much as they could have done; the master of spatial effect (Sant'Agnese, San Carlino, etc – *see pages 21* and *43*) was unable properly to adapt his talents to this building, and the end result is simply monumental. The church has many tombs and works of art: the tabernacle at the papal altar contains two particularly valuable relics: the heads of Saints Peter and Paul. The left

The gilded wood ceiling

*The cloister and
column detail*

Early Christian mosaic

transept leads to the ★★ **cloister**, where the mosaics and columns are comparable in their beauty with those in the cloister of San Paolo fuori le Mura (*see page 37*); the Cosmati decoration here dates from 1228–30.

Cosmati decoration – the name derives from several families involved in the art sharing the name Cosma – is the term used to refer to a subtle type of mosaic technique distinctive for its geometrical designs that was common in the 12th and 13th century. The colourful mosaics can be seen on choir screens, chancels, altars, episcopal thrones, candelabra and pavements. The cloisters of St John Lateran and of San Paolo fuori le Mura (*see pages 37 and 48*) contain particularly fine examples of Cosmati decoration, which declined after the transferral of the papal seat to Avignon.

We now leave the basilica of St John Lateran via the portico next to the apse, and taking the Via San Giovanni in Laterano, which starts to the left of the obelisk, we arrive at the church of ★★ **San Clemente** ❺❼ , a particularly well-preserved Early Christian basilica dating back to late antiquity. The street provides access to the 12th-century Upper Church, built in 1084 on the ruins of the first basilica (385). The three-aisled interior and the atrium with Ionic columns surrounding the little fountain are typically Early Christian. The schola cantorum (choristers' enclosure), with the two ambones (pulpits) and the marble choir screen are all from the original basilica. The Cosmati decoration on the pavement and candelabra, and also the altar mosaics, date from the 12th and 13th centuries; the ceiling was added in the 18th century. Marvellous frescoes dating from 1431 and featuring early *trompe l'oeil* effects can be admired in the chapel of St Catherine at the beginning of the left side-aisle. The sacristy next to the right-hand side-aisle provides access to the Lower Church, which was discovered in 1857; its frescoes date back to the time the Upper Church was built. The narthex contains scenes from the life of St Clement, and the Story of St Alexis (for his church, *see page 36*). A supporting wall and pillar for the Upper Church rather disturb the overall unity of this interior. The Madonna in the right-hand side-aisle (niche) and the Redeemer near the apse are both Byzantine, of uncertain date (5th–9th century).

To the left of the apse a staircase descends once again and leads to a Roman house dating from imperial times, with a Mithraic temple of the early 2nd century (*see pages 40 and 83*). The reconstructed altar shows Mithras, in his Phrygian cap, sacrificing a bull to Apollo; the stone benches in the small room were almost certainly used by the congregation. The sound of splashing water can be heard continually but its source is uncertain, and this lends the room an atmosphere of mystery; the cult of Mithras suddenly seems more real. Going back up the stairs through the Christian levels is like walking back through the millennia; no other church in the city retains this special historical dimension.

The next turn to the right off the Via San Giovanni in Laterano, the Via di Normanni, comes out into the Via Labicana and continues on its other side as a staircase leading up to the **Oppian Hill** (Mons Oppius), one of the four summits of the Esquiline.

The parkland here contains the extensive ruins of a wing of the **Domus Aurea** (Golden House) **⑱**, the luxurious palace built by Nero after the fire of AD64; it extended as far as the Roman Forum, and there was an artificial lake on the site of the Colosseum (*see page 52*). In its rooms, which today lie underground, the Laocoön was found in 1506, and the ornamental painting style in these *grotte* (caves) was called *grottesco*, from which the 'grotesque' style of painting is derived.

Crossing the Parco Oppio one then reaches the Via delle Terme di Traiano; the **Baths of Trajan ⑲**, built in the early 2nd century, were the first of their kind, and used Nero's structures as foundations. Turning left now into the Via delle Sette Sale, we arrive at the three-aisled basilica of ★ **San Pietro in Vincoli ⑳**. Sections of previous buildings dating from the 2nd century have been found below it; the present structure goes back to the year 455. The Early Renaissance facade dates from when the church was restored in 1475, and the coffered ceiling from a later restoration in 1706. The church was traditionally founded as a shrine for the chains (*vincoli*) of St Peter; the right

San Pietro in Vincoli

The Colosseum

transept contains the famous unfinished **Tomb of Julius II** by Michelangelo (1513–16), originally destined for St Peter's; the most well-known part of it, however, is Michelangelo's powerful ★★ **statue of Moses** – his most individualised work.

Beyond the church complex the Via delle Terme di Tito (named after the Baths of Titus that used to lie here) leads across the park to the ★★★ **Colosseum** (Colosseo) **61**. Vespasian began with the construction of the Colosseum, the best-preserved amphitheatre in the world, in the year AD72, on the site of the artificial lake in the gardens of Nero's Domus Aurea, in order to satisfy the Roman appetite for *panem et circenses* (bread and circuses). Countless people lost their lives during the brutal games – mainly gladiatorial combats and fights with wild beasts – which took place here. The tradition that Christians were martyred in the arena has no historical basis, however. This elliptical amphitheatre (188m/616ft long, 156m/510ft wide) with its four storeys, reaches a height of 50m (165ft) and could accommodate around 70,000 people; the interior could be covered by a huge awning, and the arena could also be flooded for mock sea-battles. Today the walls of the various dungeons, cages and passageways, gruesome reminders of the centuries-long slaughter here, can be seen through the caved-in floor of the arena.

The Colosseum became dilapidated after the fall of the Empire; in the Middle Ages it was converted into a fortress, and from the 14th century onwards was used as a quarry for building material; in the 18th century it was dedicated to the Passion of Christ, and the pope pronounced it sanctified by the blood of the martyrs; and in 1805 it was saved from collapse by the construction of a supporting wall. The columns of the Colosseum provide a fine opportunity to study the Classical Orders: Doric on the lowest storey, Ionic in the middle and Corinthian on the top, corresponding to the original design for the building. The fourth storey was added by Vespasian's successor, Titus.

Arch of Constantine

Between the Colosseum and the end of the Via dei Fori Imperiali is the triple ★ **Arch of Constantine** **62**, hastily erected in AD315 in honour of Constantine's victory over Maxentius at the Milvian Bridge (*see page 10*) three years beforehand. Some parts of the arch come from older Roman monuments, including the eight Corinthian columns, their architrave, the reliefs inside the central arch and the attic, and the eight medallions on the two facades. Despite this, however, the monument still conveys a strong sense of unity. It was modelled after the Arch of Septimius Severus in the Roman Forum (*see page 27*).

There are buses and also a Metro connection from the Colosseum back to the main station (Stazione Termini).

Route 7

★★★ St Peter's – The Vatican

The quickest route is to take Metro A from Stazione Termini to Ottaviano; the Vatican is just a short walk away down the Via Ottaviano. Bus No 64 travels from the station square to St Peter's; it ends up right next to the colonnades framing ★★★ **St Peter's Square** (Piazza San Pietro), the masterpiece of Bernini, completed in 1667. The square is in the form of a huge ellipse adjoining an almost rectangular quadrilateral, and is partly enclosed by two semicircular colonnades (symbolically embracing the city and the earth – *urbi et orbi*), each of which has a quadruple row of Doric columns (284) and pilasters (88). At the centre is an obelisk brought from Heliopolis to Rome in AD37, with fountains on either side of it that emphasise the length of the square (340m/370yds). Between the obelisk and each fountain is a round marble slab, from where the spectator obtains the illusion that each colonnade has only a single row of columns.

The cold and unattractive Via della Conciliazione leads from Castel Sant'Angelo to St Peter's Square; built by the Fascists during the 1930s, it considerably lessens the impact of Bernini's colonnaded piazza. At the end of the square above a triple flight of steps is the basilica itself, with the Vatican towering on the right. The Ionic entablature with its 140 statues of saints and martyrs completes the architectural harmony of the whole. Two 19th-century statues of the Apostles Peter and Paul stand at the foot of the great staircase leading up to the portico.

The entrance to St Peter's

St Peter's Square

★★★ St Peter's (Basilica di San Pietro)

History

The spot where the Apostle Paul was martyred and buried in AD67, during Nero's persecutions of the Christians, developed into a place of pilgrimage for Early Christianity, and after Constantine's Edict of Tolerance (AD313) a church was built on the site. The five-aisled building took the Roman architectural form of the basilica as its model, without domes but with a transept (*see page 83*); the building was consecrated by Pope Sylvester in the year 326. The tomb of St Peter, long presumed lost, was recently rediscovered during excavations beneath this original basilica. The second most important church in Christendom after that of St John Lateran (*see page 48*), St Peter's was lavishly decorated with mosaics, painting and statuary, but became so dilapidated during the course of the centuries that, despite restoration work in the 14th century, rebuilding became unavoidable.

Planning began under Pope Nicholas V (1447–55), but it was Julius II (1503–13) who decided on a complete reconstruction. He commissioned Bramante, whose plan for the new basilica was a Greek cross surmounted by a gigantic central dome. On Bramante's death in 1514, the four central piers and the arches of the dome had been completed. Raphael (died 1520) then took over, and was followed by Sangallo (died 1546); both men bowed to the clergy's wish for greater capacity by designing a nave and

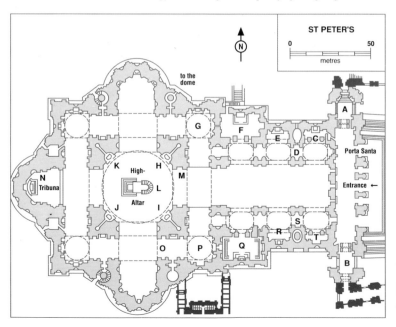

altering the ground-plan to that of a Latin cross. In 1546 however, before this could be realised, Michelangelo, then 72 years old, was summoned by Pope Paul III. He expressed his preference for the original Greek cross and central dome of Bramante; seeing the Pantheon as unambitious, though, he instead developed his own version of Brunelleschi's Florentine cupola, and substituted Bramante's piers with new ones of tremendous strength. The entire plan was finally realised after Michelangelo's death in 1564; construction work was continued until 1590 by Domenico Fontana and Giacomo Della Porta. Pope Paul V, however, now demanded a nave, and Carlo Maderna extended Michelangelo's building to give it its present-day form, adding the portico in 1614; Pope Urban VIII (1623–44) then consecrated the new building in 1626, on the 1300th anniversary of the construction of the original basilica. Seen from the square, Maderna's portico robs Michelangelo's dome of much of its power, though from a distance the cityscape is still dominated by the cupola.

Bramante's dome

Some statistics

Old basilica: church 120m (390ft) long, 64m (210ft) wide, 25m (80ft) high; entire building including atrium 220m (720ft); capacity 14,000; consecrated in AD326.

New basilica built 1506–1614: 187m (610ft) long (194m/635ft including the walls), entire building 211.5m (698ft) long. Portico 71m (230ft) wide, 13½m (44ft) deep, 20m (65ft) high; facade 114m (370ft) wide, 45m (150ft) high; nave 46m (150ft) high, 27½m (90ft) wide; transept 137½m (450ft) wide; diameter of dome 42m (137ft), overall height 132½m (434ft).

Capacity 60,000; consecrated in 1626. Number of statues: 390 (100 marble, 160 travertine, 90 stucco, 40 bronze). Number of papal tombs: 146.

Portico

Door detail, St Peter's

Eight columns and four pilasters support the entablature. The attic is almost free of decoration, and above it are statues of Christ, St John the Baptist and 11 Apostles (minus Peter), and also two clocks near the ends. The central balcony in the row of nine windows is the one from which the Pope blesses the city and the world, and from which the senior cardinal proclaims the newly-elected pontiff. Five portals lead to the vestibule, designed by Carlo Maderna; it has a very fine stucco ceiling. On the right is a statue of **Constantine** [A] by Bernini (1670), and on the left an equestrian statue of **Charlemagne** [B] (1725).

Interior

Having entered the largest church in Christendom through its central portal, one should really let the sheer immen-

Michelangelo's Pietà

Cupola interior

sity of the interior sink in, and spend some time next to the round porphyry slab set into the pavement here; it once lay in front of the altar in the original basilica, and Charlemagne knelt on it when he was crowned emperor in the year 800. The gilded barrel vault above the central nave is supported by huge pilasters; the visitor's gaze is drawn the entire length of the nave (metal lines show the various lengths of other European churches in comparison) towards the crossing, flooded with light, and the high altar at which only the Pope may celebrate. Beneath the high altar is the Tomb of St Peter, and the four 29-m (95-ft) high gilt bronze columns on plinths supporting the baldachin were designed by Bernini. On the way down the nave towards the papal altar there is a particularly fine statue, next to the fourth pilaster on the right, of the *Apostle Peter Seated* [M] by the sculptor Arnolfo di Cambio (13th-century), who introduced several Gothic sculptural elements to Rome and modelled this work after a 3rd-century philosopher statue (today in the Vatican Grottoes, *see page 59*). Further on is the holiest part of the church: the area beneath the ★★ **cupola**. Michelangelo's world-famous dome is an architectural masterpiece; it is the symbol of the city and of all Christendom.

After this general survey of the interior, we now return to the wall with the main portals. St Peter's contains literally hundreds of works of art, of which only the most important can be mentioned here. The first chapel in the right-hand side-aisle, the **Cappella della Pietà** [C], contains what is undoubtedly the most-admired work of art in the entire building: Michelangelo's exquisite ★★★ **Pietà**, which he executed at the age of 25. There is always a crowd around it. This marble sculpture, completed in the year 1500, made Michelangelo world-famous and is the only work that the artist actually inscribed with his name (the signature is on the ribbon falling from the left shoulder of the Virgin).

Directly opposite, under the first arch of the aisle, the relief on the monument to **Queen Christina of Sweden** [D] shows her renouncing the Protestant faith. Directly opposite is the Cappella San Nicola, designed by Bernini on an elliptical ground-plan, and immediately adjacent to it is the **Cappella di San Sebastiano** [E]. The large mosaic depicts the saint's martyrdom, and the monuments are to Popes Pius XI (1922–39) and Pius XII (1939–58). Under the next arch is another work by Bernini, who had a decisive hand in the interior decoration of the basilica: his monument to the Countess Matilda of Tuscany, who owned the castle in Canossa where the German emperor Henry IV did penance before Pope Gregory VII and was then secretly readmitted to the church. The **Cappella del SS Sacramento** [F] has a magnificent iron grille designed by Borromini; the gilt bronze ciborium is also another work by Bernini. The **Cappella Gregoriana** [G] was designed by Michelangelo, and its mosaic and marble decoration is Venetian.

Stoup by Bernini

Decorative details

57

We now come to the right transept of the basilica, which was used for the sessions of the First Vatican Council in 1869–70, during which the doctrine of papal infallibility was authoritatively defined under Pope Pius XI. The four pentagonal piers here support the arches on which rests the drum of the cupola. On the frieze below the drum are the words of Christ to the Apostle Peter, in 2m (6½ft) high letters: *Tu es Petrus et super hanc petram edificabo ecclesiam meam et tibi dabo claves regni coelorum* ('You are Peter and upon this rock I will build my church and I will give you the keys of the kingdom of Heaven'). Bernini decorated the four piers with niches and *loggie* using pillars from the original basilica.

The chapels contain the holiest relics in the church: the lance of **St Longinus** [H], the soldier who pierced Christ's side on the cross; the head of **St Andrew** [I], Peter's brother; the napkin of **St Veronica** [J]; and a piece of the True Cross, collected by **St Helena** [K] from Jerusalem. In front of the altar, steps lead down to the **Confessio** [L] and to the tomb of the Apostle. Here there is a marble statue by Canova of Pius V kneeling, in front of two gilded doors from the original basilica. Access to the tomb is via the Vatican Grottoes (*see page 59*).

The nave ends at the slightly raised tribune, where the most conspicuous object is the ★★ **Chair of St Peter** [N], an enormous gilt bronze throne by Bernini. It is supported by statues of the four Fathers of the Church – SS Augustine, Ambrose, Athanasius and Chrysostom – and encloses

St Veronica

an ancient wooden chair inlaid with ivory, which is said to have been the episcopal chair of St Peter. Angels and putti surround a halo of gilt stucco, with a key symbolising Heaven and a dove symbolising the Holy Spirit. Bernini completed this very ambitious composition in 1665. There are two magnificent monuments next to it: to the right, the ★★ **monument to Pope Urban VIII**, also by Bernini, and to the left, the ★★ **monument to Pope Paul III** by Giacomo Della Porta.

The way back via the left-hand side-aisle begins with the monument to **Pius VIII** [O], a 19th-century work. The entrance to the Sacristy and the Treasury (Tesoro di San Pietro) can also be found here. On the right-hand side of the vestibule there is a large stone slab on which is inscribed the names of the popes buried in the basilica. Highlights of the treasury include: the *Dalmatic of Charlemagne*, which he is supposed to have worn for his coronation, and the 6th-century *Crux Vaticana*, a gift from the emperor Justinian II (565–78).

Detail, Capella Clementina

58

Next along the left-hand side-aisle is the **Cappella Clementina** [P]; Pope Gregory the Great lies buried under the altar here. The adjacent monument to Pius VII is by the neoclassical Danish sculptor Thorwaldsen (1823). The lavishly decorated **Cappella del Coro** [Q] contains one of the most important works of art in the church, and the only monument from the old basilica to be recreated in the new: the bronze ★★ monument to Innocent VIII (1484–92) by the sculptor Antonio Pollaiuolo (1498). It was the first monument to show a pope sitting on his throne.

After the monument to Pius X (canonised in 1954) comes the **Cappella della Presentazione** [R], containing the monument to Benedict XV (1914–22), and also a relief depicting John XXIII preaching. Past the **entrance to the dome** [S] is the **Cappella Battistero** [T]; the font is actually the cover of a porphyry sarcophagus placed upside down. Its magnificent bronze cover is the work of Carlo Fontana.

The view from the balustrade

★★ **Dome**: A lift and also a staircase lead up to the roof and the dome of St Peter's from the courtyard outside the church on the right (turn right out of the portico through the grille door and then immediately left beyond it, *see Plan, page 54*); descent and exit is at [S]. There is a fine view of St Peter's Square from the balustrade on the facade. There are two circular galleries between the inner and outer walls of the cupola, the lower one is 53m (170ft) up, the higher one 73m (240ft), providing a good view of the mosaics and of the high altar. From the lantern, 123m (400ft) up, there is a superb view of the entire city and surrounding countryside.

At night the dome is illuminated by a pale blue light, while a pastel pink light bathes the basilica.

The Vatican

★★ Vatican Grottoes

The entrance to the Sacre Grotte Vaticane (they occupy the space between the level of the existing basilica and that of the old one) is either at the pier of St Longinus or the pier of St Andrew (it varies). The floor is actually the ceiling of the earlier basilica. Excavations carried out beneath the older church have revealed a filled-in necropolis dating from antiquity, and also what appears to be St Peter's Tomb, near the site of the Circus of Nero, the most likely place of his martyrdom (access to necropolis only with special permission). The most important work of art in the Grottoes is Pollaiuolo's monument to Sixtus IV (1471–84), who founded the Vatican Museums and also gave his name to the Sistine Chapel (see page 65). The richly-decorated ★ **Cappella Clementina** lies above the presumed Tomb of St Peter.

Vatican postbox

The Vatican State

The smallest state in the world – Stato della Città del Vaticano – covers a surface area of just 440,000sq m (526,240sq yds), 55,000 (65,780) of which are taken up by St Peter's; of its 900 or so inhabitants, roughly 550 are Vatican citizens. The Vatican today is the seat and

59

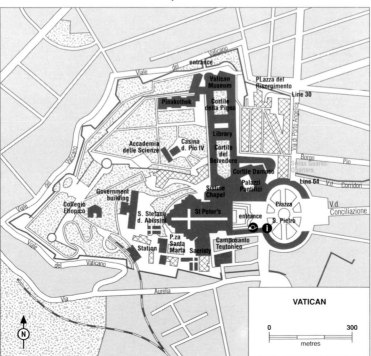

administrative centre of the Roman Catholic Church. It has its own post office, railway station, bank, newspaper (*Osservatore Romano*) and radio station. The head of state is the Pope, and the cardinals of the Curia are in effect his ministers. The army of more than 100 Swiss Guards – whose picturesque uniforms were designed by Michelangelo – look after security. The City has no income tax and no restriction on the import or export of funds; banking operations are veiled in secrecy. The Vatican in its present form has been in existence since 1929. The loss of the Papal States in 1870 (*see page 11*) was compensated for by the new Italian state (under the terms of the Lateran Treaty of 1929) in the form of substantial sums of money, which the church duly invested in international finance. The Vatican state also has some extraterritorial possessions alongside Vatican City including several churches in Rome and also the papal summer residence of Castel Gandolfo.

Swiss Guard

Stera con stera sculpture,
Vatican Palace

60

View of the Vatican
from St Peter's

The Vatican Palace

The Lateran Palace (*see page 48*), the seat of the papacy since the time of Constantine, was destroyed when the popes returned to Rome from Avignon, and construction work began on a new palace on the site of today's Vatican in 1377. The popes had always had a house near the basilica of St Peter, and during antiquity the area, known as the *ager vaticanus*, lay outside Rome's city walls. The emperor Nero then had a circus built, in which St Peter was martyred, and St Peter's basilica was built above the Apostle's tomb (*see page 54*). Today's Vatican Palace dates from 1450. The sections of it to the north of St Peter's –

the Appartamento Borgia, the Stanze and the Sistine Chapel – date from the second half of the 15th century. The Belvedere, originally a pavilion, was completed in 1492. The alterations carried out by Domenico Fontana between 1585 and 1590 resulted in the sections that still enclose the Cortile del Belvedere (main courtyard) and the Cortile della Pigna (Courtyard of the Fir-Cone) today; the Braccio Nuovo (New Wing), between the Library and the Cortile della Pigna, was added in 1822. The neoclassical rooms north of the Cortile della Pigna, housing the Vatican collections of antiquities, were built at the end of the 18th century. The Picture Gallery dates from 1932, and in 1963 Pope John XXIII had a new museum building (opened by Paul VI in 1970) constructed alongside it to house the collections from the Lateran Palace.

Papal audiences, admission for visitors
Assuming the Pope is in Rome, the official papal audience takes place every Wednesday around 11am in St Peter's Square, and in summer and winter in the Paul V Assembly Hall; on Sunday after 12 noon he delivers his blessing from the window of his study (palace on the right beyond the colonnades). Special audiences have to be applied for in writing or in person from the Prefetto della Casa Pontificia del Palazzo Apostolico, I-00120 Città del Vaticano, Tuesday 9am–1pm. The following sights in Vatican City may be visited without a permit: St Peter's, the Vatican Museums and also the Campo Santo Teutonico (German cemetery), reached via the portal to the left of the basilica facade. Special permission is necessary for access to other buildings and the Vatican Gardens. Information available from: Ufficio Informazioni Pellegrini e Turisti, Piazza San Pietro (in the colonnade on the left in front of the basilica).

★★★ Vatican Museums
Opening hours: 9am–5pm July, August, September and during Easter; 9am–2pm other months (closed Sunday).

Vatican museums

The visitors' entrance to the Vatican Museums is a short distance up the Viale Vaticano, which branches off the Piazza del Risorgimento. The Vatican bus service runs from the Arco delle Campane (left of the basilica) through the Vatican gardens to a side-entrance to the Museums, at the Ambulatory, and is also a good way of seeing part of the city and gardens. The sheer size and complexity of the Vatican Museums and the enormous number of exhibits have made the museum authorities organise a system of four routes (A, B, C, D) marked in different colours; all of them, including the shortest one (about 1½ hours), include the most important sights as well as the Sistine

Admiring the treasures

Chapel. Because different visitors have different tastes and because of the vast amount of exhibits, no single route is described here since there is plenty of detailed information available at the entrance; instead, individual sections are named and their chief works of art listed. Do allow at least half a day, though, for even the most cursory look at the collections here.

★★ **Gregorian Museum of Pagan Antiquities** (Musei di Antichità). These collections are the largest in the world, and are housed in the building between the Cortile della Pigna and the Vatican Wall, on the left of the main entrance to the Museums.

Bronze statue of Hercules

The ★★ **Museo Pio-Clementino** sculpture gallery is divided up into the following sections:

Hall of the Greek Cross (Sala a Croce Greca): porphyry sarcophagi of the emperor Constantine's mother and daughter, St Helena and Constantia.

Circular Hall (Sala Rotonda): colossal gilded bronze statue of Hercules; colossal head of Jupiter of Otricoli, a Roman copy of the Greek original (4th-century BC).

Hall of the Muses (Sala delle Muse): statues of Apollo and the nine Muses; in the centre of the hall, the *Belvedere Torso* (1st-century BC), a Greek work admired greatly by Raphael and Michelangelo.

Animal Room (Sala degli Animali): remarkable animal statues by Antonio Franzoni (1734–1818), after Roman originals; *Meleager with his Dog and the Head of a Boar*, a copy of a Greek original by Skopas (4th-century BC).

Gallery of Statues (Galleria delle Statue): Roman copies of Greek originals, including *Apollo Sauroctonos* (lizard-killer) after the original by Praxiteles (4th-century BC).

Gallery of Busts (Galleria dei Busti): Roman busts.

The Mask Room (Gabinetto delle Maschere): mosaics (2nd-century AD) of theatrical masks in the pavement, brought from Hadrian's Villa; the *Venus of Knidos*, a copy of the statue by Praxiteles (4th-century BC).

Octagonal Courtyard of the Belvedere (Cortile del Belvedere, not to be confused with the larger one to the south): famous group of *Laocoön* and his two sons (Greek, 1st-century BC); *Apollo Belvedere* (a Roman copy).

Gabinetto dell'Apoxyomenos: statue of an athlete known as *Apoxyomenos* (The Scraper), a Roman copy of a work by Lysippos (4th century BC).

Bramante's staircase

After this room a fine ★ **staircase** by Bramante leads up to the ★ **Etruscan Museum** (Museo Gregoriano Etrusco), containing many finds including those from the Regolini-Galassi Tomb near Cerveteri; Greek, Italic and Etruscan vases; and the *Mars of Todi* (bronze, 4th-century BC).

Egyptian Museum (Museo Gregoriano Egizio). Ten rooms here provide a good overall impression of the history of Egyptian art, albeit mostly via copies from later eras and also reconstructions.

Egyptian exhibit

The Chiaramonti Gallery (Museo Chiaramonti) contains Greek and Roman sculpture; the New Wing (Braccio Nuovo), south of the Cortile della Pigna, houses the *Augustus of Prima Porta*, a famous 1st-century Roman original; the *Resting Satyr*, a copy of a work by Praxiteles; and *The Nile*, a fine Hellenistic work.

The ★★ **Vatican Library** (*Biblioteca Apostolica Vaticana*). Founded by Nicholas V in 1450, it contains some of the most priceless works in the world including 60,000 manuscripts, some 7,000 incunabula, and around half a million printed books. The library's Museum of Pagan Antiquities is in Bramante's west corridor; the Sistine Hall (Sala Sistina) contains an exhibition of valuable manuscripts and printed books.

The **Museum of Christian Art** (Museo Sacro) contains the results of excavations carried out in the catacombs and below the Early Christian churches.

63

The Sala dei Papiri and the Sala degli Indirizzi lead into the Hall of the Aldobrandini Marriage, named after the famous painting here dating from the time of the emperor Augustus, which is actually a Roman copy of a Greek original (4th-century BC). The fresco was found on the Esquiline in 1605.

Borgia Rooms (Appartamento Borgia): Borgia Pope Alexander VI (1492–1503) lived in these six apartments and had them decorated with frescoes by Bernardino Pinturicchio and his pupils; apart from Room VI (Sala dei Pontefici) they have remained intact.

1 *Sala del Sibille*: paintings of sibyls and prophets.

2 *Sala del Credo*: the 12 Apostles of the Church holding scrolls with sentences from the Creed, and accompanied by prophets.

3 *Sala delle Arti Liberali*: allegories of the seven Liberal Arts (grammar, dialectics, rhetoric, geometry, arithmetic, music and astronomy).

4 *Sala della Vita dei Santi*: the ★ **frescoes** by Pinturicchio portraying scenes from the lives of the saints here are considered his greatest achievement, and are the undisputed highlight of the Borgia Rooms.

5 *Sala dei Misteri*: depictions of Mysteries of the Faith (the pope kneeling in the *Resurrection* is Alexander VI).

6 *Sala dei Pontefici (Room of the Popes)*: Stucco, frescoes and tapestries.

***Raphael Rooms** (Stanze di Raffaello). It was Pope Julius II (1503–13) who commissioned Raphael to decorate these four rooms. The artist worked on them until his death in 1520; his pupils then completed their master's greatest achievement.

1 *Stanza dell'Incendio* (Fire in the Borgo rooms): The only work here by Raphael is the *Incendio di Borgo* (Fire in the Borgo), illustrating the fire that broke out in Rome in 847; ceiling frescoes are by Perugino, Raphael's teacher; the other frescoes are by his pupil, Giulio Romano.

Fire in Borgo

2 *Stanza della Segnatura*: This was the first room to be entirely painted by Raphael, and is generally considered his greatest achievement. The ceiling medallions contain allegories of Justice, Theology, Philosophy and Poetry – themes that are further developed in the frescoes decorating the wall.

The Triumph of Justice on the wall above the window is depicted by the three Cardinal Virtues (Fortitude, Temperance and Prudence) and also by the pope handing the Decretals to a jurist to represent Canon Law. The Triumph of Poetry depicts the Parnassus, with Apollo surrounded by the nine Muses and the great poets (including Homer, Dante and Virgil, and also Boccaccio, Petrarch, Ariosto and Sappho).

64

To depict the Triumph of Philosophy, Raphael chose the School of Athens as his subject, a gathering of the great minds of antiquity; the bearded Plato in the middle (thought to be intended as a portrait of Leonardo da Vinci), Euclid (with the features of Bramante) and in the centre foreground the seated figure of Heraclitus (with the features of Michelangelo); the man with the black hat in the right-hand corner is Raphael himself.

Decorative detail, Raphael Rooms

On the long wall opposite the entrance is the famous *Disputa del Sacramento*, a glorification of Catholicism and of the Triumph of the Church. On the right of the saints and doctors of the Church in the terrestrial section the head of Dante crowned by laurel can be seen, and beyond him in a black hat is Savonarola; on the extreme left is Fra Angelico wearing a black Dominican habit, and in the foreground is Bramante.

3 *Stanza d'Eliodoro*: Four large paintings here depict historical scenes; Raphael may not have painted everything himself. Opposite the entrance is *The Expulsion of Heliodorus from the Temple*. On the long wall is *Leo I Repulsing Attila*, an allusion to the battle of Ravenna in 1512 where Leo X drove the French out of Italy.

Opposite the window is a depiction of the *Deliverance of St Peter*; the light effects of these night scenes are justly famous. The *Mass of Bolsena* recounts the famous miracle of 1263, when a priest who had doubts about the doctrine of transubstantiation suddenly saw blood issue from the host at the moment of the sacrifice, and was duly convinced.

4 *Sala di Costantino*: These frescoes depicting scenes from the life of Constantine the Great were painted after Raphael's death in 1520, mostly by Giulio Romano, one of his pupils.

Chapel of Nicholas V (Cappella di Niccolò V): The ★ **frescoes** here are by Fra Angelico (1448–50), and represent scenes from the lives of saints Stephen and Laurence. They are among his finest works.

Loggia of Raphael: This long, 13-bay gallery was started by Bramante and completed by Raphael and his pupils, who painted it with 48 scenes from the Old Testament and 4 scenes from the New (it is also known as the 'Raphael Bible'). There is a fine view from the Loggia of Bramante's magnificent Courtyard of St Damasus (Cortile di Damaso).

★★★ **Sistine Chapel** (Cappella Sistina): This 40-m (130-ft) long, 13-m (42-ft) wide and 20-m (65-ft) high room was built under Sixtus IV (1473–84) as the official private chapel of the popes. Between 1481 and 1483 its walls were painted by the most celebrated artists of the day (including Botticelli, Ghirlandaio and Perugino). The chapel was restored in 1993.

The southern wall, with scenes from the life of Moses, has its counterpart in the scenes from the life of Christ on the north wall. The barrel-vaulted ceiling, which originally depicted a starry sky, was painted by Michelangelo between 1508 and 1512 at the request of Pope Julius

65

Sistine Chapel ceiling

II. Nine rectangular panels along the centre of the vault depict scenes from Genesis, from the Creation to events in the life of Noah.

In the lunettes over the windows are figures representing the forerunners of Christ, with sybils and prophets at their sides (each lunette was painted in just three days, directly on to the fresh plaster, without the help of a preliminary cartoon).

Between 1536 and 1541 Michelangelo (then in his sixties) decorated the altar end with a massive fresco of the *Last Judgement*. His revolutionary, anti-authoritarian depiction of the saints as nude figures, and the enigmatic, beardless figure of Christ incurred much criticism and indignation from the clergy. Pius IV nevertheless decided against destroying this great masterpiece; instead, he ordered Daniel da Volterra to paint garments on a number of the figures.

Galleria delle Carte – Map gallery

Picture gallery entrance

Galleria delle Carte Geografiche, Galleria dei Candelabri e degli Arazzi: Along Bramante's 120-m (390-ft) long West Gallery which runs from the Sistine Chapel back to the entrance, visitors have the chance to see 40 painted maps of Italy dating from the late 16th century. There are also tapestries woven in Brussels with scenes from the life of Christ, executed after Raphael's death by his pupils and based on his cartoons; marble candelabra from imperial Rome, and several statues and magnificent sculptures.

Picture Gallery (Pinacoteca): This gallery, which contains the Vatican painting collections, is reached via the passageway from the open court beyond the Quattro Cancelli; it was founded by Pius VI (1775–99).

This huge collection of paintings from Byzantine times to the present includes several masterpieces by the following artists: Giotto and his pupils (room 3); Fra Angelico (room 3); Melozzo da Forli (room 4); Raphael (room 8); Leonardo da Vinci (room 9); Titian and others (room 10); Caravaggio, Domenichino (room 12).

Museo Gregoriano Profano: Antique sculpture (Roman originals and copies of Greek originals).

Museo Missionario-Etnologico: Over 3,000 exhibits in this museum illustrate the way of life and customs in China, Polynesia, Persia, Africa, South and Central America, and Australia.

Museo Storico: This museum was founded by Paul VI, and exhibits include weapons, uniforms and coaches, all documenting Vatican history.

Route 8

Street near Via Giulia

A tram-ride around Rome: Piazza del Risorgimento – ★ Trastevere – ★ Janiculum (*see Map, pages 14/15*)

67

Visiting the Vatican can be rather tiring, but one good way of combining duty with pleasure is to take a No 30 tram directly from the Vatican – it'll take you almost right round the city in comfort. The terminus of line 30 is on the Piazza del Risorgimento right next to the Vatican Wall; 800 lire or so will provide you with a colourful impression of the Rome of yesterday and today. The first district of the city the tram goes through is the **Prati**, laid out in 1880, with its slightly neoclassical-looking facades and shady shopping avenues. The Via delle Milizie leads to the Tiber, which the tram crosses at the Matteotti Bridge. Passing the *Via Flaminia*, the ancient Roman road to Rimini, the tram then travels along the edge of the city's large and popular park, the ★★ **Villa Borghese**, also passing the Villa Giulia, which houses the National Museum of Etruscan Art. The trip now continues past the National Gallery of Modern Art (Galleria Nazionale d'Arte Moderna) and also the Zoo (Giardine Zoologico). The park now turns into a leafy residential area. Here Italian architects, conscious of the city's rich artistic heritage, have livened up the facades of the apartment buildings with gable-windows and geometrical decoration.

Tram No 30

A good half-hour later the tram reaches the Policlinico and the Città Universitaria, both of them purpose-built. Tram No 30 turns round now and heads back for the city centre; at this point, though, it's worth breaking the journey to visit the church of ★ **San Lorenzo fuori le Mura**, one of the seven pilgrimage churches of Rome. It dates back to the Early Christian period. Today's restored interior and the portico are 13th-century; the simple cam-

A statue in Villa Borghese Park

panile is one century older, as is the magnificent cloister. The earlier basilica is on a different level; the raised chancel dates from the 6th century. The church's narthex is now the mausoleum of Pius IX (1864–78). Excavations beneath the church have revealed finds dating from the 3rd century; St Laurence, the church's patron saint, was martyred in the year 258.

The tram now travels from the Piazzale San Lorenzo through a less attractive district. At the Porta Maggiore is the curious *Tomb of the Baker Marcus Virgilius Eurysaces* (c 30BC), built in the form of an oven. Above is a frieze illustrating the various stages of bread-making. Next comes another of the 'Seven Churches', **Santa Croce in Gerusalemme**. The empress Helena brought back relics of the True Cross with her from Jerusalem in the 3rd century, and this church was built to house them; it was completely modernised by Benedict XIV in 1744. This route affords repeated glimpses of the Aurelian Wall, which is remarkably well-preserved in this section of the city. At the basilica of San Giovanni in Laterano (*see page 48*) the tramline now heads off towards the city centre and the Colosseum (*see page 52*) before crossing an area of parkland to reach the Circus Maximus.

Santa Maria in Trastevere

The Tempietto in San Pietro in Montorio

At the Porta San Paolo (*see page 36*) you can either take the Metro back to the city centre or take a stroll along the Via Marmorata and across the Ponte Sublicio to Trastevere. Just before the bridge there is a superb view of the Aventine Hill across to the right; after crossing the bridge, go past the Porta Portese (popular flea-market here on Sundays) to reach ★ **Trastevere**. The name means 'beyond the Tiber', and the Via San Francesco a Ripa branches off to the left to reach the church of ★ **Santa Maria in Trastevere**, which was probably the first church in Rome to be dedicated to the Virgin. The present structure dates from the 12th century, and the portico was built in 1702. The stucco ceiling was designed by Domenichino (1617); the ★ **mosaics** (c 1291) in the apse depicting the Life of Mary are by Pietro Cavallini. There is a bus connection from here back to the centre, but this picturesque old quarter of the city deserves further exploration. From Santa Maria in Trastevere the Via di Paglia and the Via Garibaldi lead uphill to the church of **San Pietro in Montorio**, the courtyard of which contains the magnificent ★ **Tempietto** by Bramante (dating from 1499–1502), erected on the supposed exact site of St Peter's martyrdom. This fine round temple is one of the finest examples of High Renaissance architecture. There is a superb view of Rome's city centre from the square in front of the church.

Further uphill on the Via Garibaldi is the fountain of the **Acqua Paola**, built in the form of a triumphal arch by Carlo Maderna (1612), who received the commission from

Paul V (hence the name). A little further up, the Passeggiata del Gianicolo branches off to the right. Walk along this leafy promenade across the elongated hill known as the ★ **Janiculum** (Gianicolo) as far as the Piazzale Garibaldi with its monument to the famous freedom-fighter (1895). There is a magnificent panoramic view of all Rome from the terrace up here. Going back down the Passeggiata del Gianicolo, a flight of steps to the left and then a steep road lead back down to the Via Garibaldi. At the end of it on the left, just a few steps along the Via della Lungara, are the Botanical Gardens (Orto Botanico). Next to them is the **Palazzo Corsini**, which houses the ★★ **Galleria Nazionale dei Lincei** with its magnificent collection of 17th- and 18th-century paintings (open Monday to Friday 9am–2pm, Sunday 9am–1pm).

Interior, Palazzo Corsini

Opposite the palazzo, in a park, is the ★ **Villa Farnesina** (closed Sunday). This two-storey structure was built between 1508 and 1511, and was decorated by several famous artists under the direction of Raphael. It was here that the owner, a banker named Agostino Chigi, held lavish banquets at which each guest was given silver plates and dishes, which after the meal were thrown into the Tiber (although it was later discovered that the wily banker had placed a net there in order to recover them). The first floor contains several erotic Renaissance paintings: Sodoma painted an ★ *Alexander's Wedding* for the bedroom; it is surrounded by much *trompe l'oeil* decoration. Two works by Raphael on erotic themes in the garden gallery, his ★ *Legend of Cupid and Psyche* and the celebrated *Galatea*, are true masterpieces.

Turn left when leaving the Villa Farnesina, and the Via della Lungara (this area has several fine restaurants, by the way) leads to the Porta Settimiana. The Tiber is just a short walk away to the left; cross the Ponte Sisto and you will find yourself back in the historic city centre.

Bridge over the Tiber

Statues on the Gianicolo

Santa Maria del Popolo

Route 9

Piazza del Popolo – ★ Pincio – ★ Villa Borghese – Via Vittorio Veneto – Piazza Barberini

The Piazza del Popolo provides a picturesque entrance to the city from the Via Flaminia and the north. The **Porta del Popolo** ㉓ used to be part of the Aurelian Wall; the outer face of the gate was designed by Michelangelo and executed by Vignola, and the inner face is by Bernini. An obelisk from Heliopolis (found buried in the Circus Maximus) was erected in the centre of the square in 1585, and surrounded by a fountain with lions. In the 17th century two baroque churches, Santa Maria di Monte Santo and Santa Maria dei Miracoli, were added at the top of the Corso (*see page 73*), and during the Napoleonic era Valadier gave the square its present symmetry by adding the two semicircular sections opposite the Tiber and the Pincio.

Next to the Porta del Popolo is the church of ★ **Santa Maria del Popolo** ㉔, which dates from the time of Sixtus IV (1472–84), and has an Early Renaissance facade.

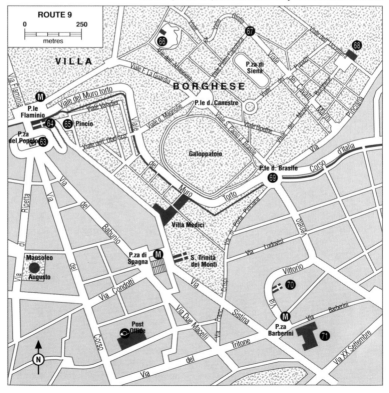

The baroque ornamentation at the sides was added by Bernini, who also 'baroque-ised' the interior (c 1658). As well as containing several fine Renaissance and baroque works of art, the church is the burial-place of many popes. Artistic highlights here include, in the chapel to the left of the main altar, *The Conversion of St Paul* and *The Crucifixion of St Peter* (1602) by Caravaggio, and also the frescoes by Pinturicchio (1454–1513) in the apse, which was designed by Bramante. The church's octagonal ★ **Chigi Chapel**, founded by the great banker Chigi (*see page 69*), was designed by Raphael.

Fresco by Pinturicchio

There are two delightful ways of getting up to the park known as the ★ **Pincio** from here: either via the stairs outside the church's side-exit, or along the Viale Gabriele d'Annunzio. The terrace on the **Piazzale Napoleone 65** affords one of the finest views of Rome; the historic centre and Vatican City on the opposite bank of the Tiber lie at your feet; the architecture of the generously-proportioned Piazza del Popolo, with the streets radiating out from it, becomes clear; and there is a superb view of all the domed buildings of Rome, starting with the cupola of Santa Maria del Popolo, the oldest in the city.

The terrace here is part of the ★ **Villa Borghese**, Rome's most famous public park. It was bought by the state in 1902 and handed over to the City of Rome. From the terrace the Viale dell'Obelisco and the Viale delle Magnolie lead to the Piazzale delle Canestre; turn left here to reach the **Giardino del Lago 66**, where a copy of a **Greek temple** (that of Aesculapius) can be seen on a small island. The Via di Valle Giulia leads past the 16th-century La Fortezzuola to the delightful **Temple of Faustina 67**; nearby is the attractive Piazza di Siena, a rustic amphitheatre where equestrian events and festivals are held.

The Greek Temple

The Viale dei Cavalli Marini now intersects with the Viale del Museo Borghese; a little further on is a villa housing the ★★ **Museo and Galleria Borghese 68**; it was built by Scipio Borghese in 1613 to house his art collection; in 1833 the collection, which is first-class, became the property of the state. On the first floor are paintings by the most famous Italian masters of the 16th and 17th centuries: Perugino, Botticelli, Raphael, Caravaggio, and also Titian (*Sacred and Profane Love*, his early masterpiece). The ground floor contains several antique statues and also numerous important works by Bernini (including *David* and *Truth*) and also by Antonio Canova (*Paolina Borghese*). Opening hours: Monday to Saturday 9am–2pm, Sunday 9am–1pm; only ground floor accessible at present.

A Caravaggio in Galleria Borghese

From the gallery the route leads directly to the **Porta Pinciana 69**, beyond which the famous Via Vittorio Veneto begins. The Via Veneto was especially fashionable in the 1950s and 1960s for its *La Dolce Vita* ambience;

Fontana del Tritone

'I made the film, and then everyone started copying it,' Fellini remarked. Nothing of that decadence remains today. The street is now lined with hotels, cafés and expensive boutiques. Just before the Piazza Barberini is the church of **Santa Maria della Concezione ⑦**, also known as the Church of the Cappuccini; there is a rather gruesome museum on its lower level (open daily 9am–1pm and 3–7pm). The bones and skeletons of the 4,000 or so corpses in the Capuchin Cemetery below the church have been arranged in patterns, according to Spanish custom.

The Piazza Barberini, where the Via Veneto ends, contains a fine fountain by Bernini: his ★ **Fontana del Tritone** (1632–7), in the form of a shell with dolphins and a Triton spouting water into the air. Another fountain by Bernini is on the corner with Via Veneto: the Bee Fountain, featuring a bee of science-fiction dimensions, immortalising the Barberini coat-of-arms.

A short way beyond it is the most important baroque palazzo in Rome, the ★★ **Palazzo Barberini ⑦**, on which Maderna, Bernini and Borromini all worked between 1632 and 1637. This was the family palace of Pope Urban VIII, and is sumptuously decorated. In the large salon, Pietro da Cortona created what is considered one of the most important frescoes of high baroque, the *Triumph of Providence*.

Portrait of a gentleman by Veneto

Wayside attractions

The Palazzo Barberini houses the ★★ **Galleria Nazionale d'Arte Antica**, with Italian masters from the 13th to 16th century and also French masters of the 18th and 19th centuries. Fra Angelico, Filippo Lippi, Perugino, El Greco, Tintoretto, Raphael, Veneto, and many more are all represented here (open Monday to Saturday 9am–2pm, Sunday 9am–1pm).

Route 10

Piazza del Popolo – Via del Corso – Mausoleum of Augustus – ★★ Ara Pacis Augustae – ★ Piazza Borghese – Via della Scrofa – ★ Sant'Agostino – ★ Via dei Coronari – ★ Castel Sant'Angelo

The Via del Corso, or *Il Corso* as it is affectionately known, connects the Piazza del Popolo with the ★ Piazza Venezia, and is one of the main thoroughfares of present-day Rome. Historically, the Corso is actually an extension of the old *Via Flaminia*. It was named after the celebrated races that were held here until the end of the last century. At the top of the Corso are two 17th-century churches: the one on the left is **Santa Maria di Monte Santo ⑫**, with its lantern by Bernini, and the one on the right is **Santa Maria**

Santa Maria di Monte Santo

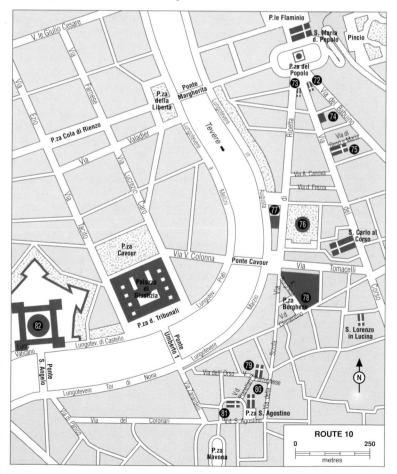

Santi Ambrogio e Carlo al Corso

Mercato delle Stampe

dei Miracoli **73**, with its 18th-century campanile. On the left-hand side of the street, house No 18 is the **Casa di Goethe** **74**, where the famous poet stayed with his painter friend Tischbein during his stay in Rome. He memorably describes the Corso and the horse-race in his *Italian Journey*.

The 17th-century church of **Gesù e Maria** **75**, one of those highly attractive Roman churches built on elliptical ground-plans, stands in the side-street of the same name. The polychromatic marble interior is attributed to Maderna; the successful facade is by Rainaldi. **Santi Ambrogio e Carlo al Corso**, on the other side of the street, has one of the largest domes in the city. A small street just to the right of it leads to the Piazza Augusto Imperatore, a junction of several bus lines. The square gets its name from the **Mausoleum of Augustus** **76**, a colossal round building measuring 87m (285ft) in diameter, and originally 44m (145ft) in height. This tomb of Augustus and of the principal members of his family was one of the most sacred monuments of ancient Rome; it was erected in 28BC, and has had quite a chequered history. In the Middle Ages it was a fortress, and today it is a ruin. The crypt is closed to the public.

On the opposite side of the street in the direction of the Tiber is the ★★ **Ara Pacis** **77**, Augustus's peace altar, consecrated in 9BC and reconstructed in 1938. After several successful campaigns in Spain and Gaul, Augustus announced an era of peace, the *Pax Augustea*. The reliefs on the Ara Pacis show just how sophisticated sculpture had become under imperial Rome. Opening hours: daily except Monday 9am–1.30pm; Tuesday, Thursday and Saturday 4–7pm (in summer); Sunday 9am–1pm.

The Via di Ripetta (*ripa* means riverbank) is a reminder of the former harbour here when ships plied the Tiber. It joins the Via della Scrofa, from which the first left turn, the Via Borghese, leads to the ★ **Piazza Borghese**, dominated by the impressive facade of the ★ **Palazzo Borghese** **78**, built in around 1600. Its ground-plan is reminiscent of a harpsichord, which is why the facade-side is often referred to as *la tastiera* (the keyboard). The inner courtyard here is definitely worth a visit: 96 columns in two storeys, with Rainaldi's *Bagno di Venere* rococo fountain (1680) contrasting well with the severity of the Renaissance architecture. On weekdays, the **Mercato delle Stampe**, a picturesque book and antiques fair, is held in the piazza, where there are usually bargains to be had.

The Via del Clementino now leads on to the Via della Scrofa, which lies at the centre of a commercial district with lots of small shops. Down the Via dei Portoghesi to the right is the tiny baroque church of **Sant'Antonio dei Portoghesi** **79**, the former church of the Portuguese in

Rome (early 17th-century). The Via dei Pianellari directly opposite leads to the church of ★ **Sant'Agostino** . The garage built into its lower floor is typical of the city's careless attitude towards its monuments.

A broad flight of steps leads up to one of the first Renaissance facades in Rome (1479–83), its three portals leading to the three-aisled interior. On the high altar by Bernini (1627) is a Byzantine Madonna brought from Constantinople. The tomb of St Monica, St Augustine's mother, is in the chapel to the left. She died in 387. On the inside of the main portal is one of the most highly revered statues in the city, the *Madonna del Parto*, a work by Sansovino (1521). The first chapel in the left-hand side-aisle contains the *Madonna dei Pellegrini* by Caravaggio (1605), and on the third pillar on the north side is a fresco of the prophet *Isaiah* by Raphael (1512).

From the piazza in front of the church the Via Sant'Agostino opens out on to the Piazza Sant'Apollinare with the church of **Sant'Apollinare** ❸. Its portico contains ★ *La Madonna del Portico* (Umbrian school, 15th-century), a fresco depicting the Madonna and Child flanked by saints Peter and Paul. The ★ **Via dei Coronari** here and its side-streets make up what is perhaps the most picturesque quarter in the historic city centre: antiques shops, small restaurants, peaceful arcades. It ends at the Piazza dei Coronari; the Tiber and the ★ **Ponte Sant'Angelo** are only a few steps away.

The latter was built by Hadrian in AD136 as a fitting approach to his mausoleum. Its 16th- and 17th-century statues make it one of the most attractive of Rome's ancient bridges: the Apostles Peter and Paul at the entrance date from 1530, and the 10 angels by Bernini and his school (two are copies of originals in Sant'Andrea delle Fratte) were added in 1688. The central three arches are part of the original structure.

The ★★ **Castel Sant'Angelo** ❽ was originally built by Hadrian as the sepulchre for himself and his family in AD135–39, and was modelled on the tomb of Mausolus at Halicarnassos, one of the Seven Wonders of the World. In the Middle Ages it was used as a fortress, a prison and a royal residence; damaged several times, it was repeatedly rebuilt. This 20-m (65-ft) high cylindrical structure stands on a base measuring 84m (275ft) square, and today is a museum (open Monday 2–6pm, Tuesday to Saturday 9am–2pm, Sunday 9am–1pm). The various rooms inside the building (papal chambers, weapons collections, historic documentation) are accessible via the 125-m (410-ft) long spiral ramp inside, which is still in an excellent state of preservation. At the top of the ramp is the ★ **terrace**, with its superb view. The huge **bronze angel** was placed here in 1753.

Flower stall

75

The Ponte and Castel Sant'Angelo

The bronze angel

Theatre, Ostia Antica

Three Excursions outside the City

1. Ostia

Leave Rome by car at the Porta San Paolo and the 28-km (17-miles) long *autostrada* will take you to Lido di Roma (Ostia), which can also be reached by public transport (Metro, train; *see page 96*). Today the ancient Roman harbour city of **Ostia Antica** is 3km (2 miles) away from the sea. Founded in the 4th century BC, it had 50,000 inhabitants during imperial times. The excavations here, ★★ **Scavi di Ostia Antica**, provide a fascinating glimpse into the history of the city (open daily except Monday 9am–dusk).

Mosaics and street in Ostia Antica

The **Porta Romana** [A] still contains remains of the gate from the Republican period; it stands at the beginning of the 1-km long *Decumano Massimo*, the road that led to the actual harbour.

On the **Piazzale della Vittoria** [B] stands a colossal statue of Minerva Victoria (1st century BC), and opposite lie the **Horrea** [C], or warehouses, and the **Terme di Nettuno** [D] with magnificent 2nd-century ★ **mosaics**. Later on the same side of the street are the **Palaestra** [E], or gymnasium, and the **Caserma dei Vigili** [F] (Firemen's Barracks, 2nd-century AD). On the other side of the street and set back slightly are the **Horrea di Hortensius** [G] (warehouses), and then on the right comes the reconstructed **Teatro** [H] built by Agrippa, and restored by Septimius Severus and Caracalla in the 3rd century. The theatre is a semicircular building of the usual Roman type; the proscenium and marble niches are antique. Classical music performances take place here in the summer months. The top rows of seats provide a view across the ★ **Piazzale delle Corporazioni** (Square of the Guilds) with the **Tempio di Cerere** [I] in the middle. This commercial centre

once contained 70 offices of associations ranging from workers' guilds to foreign representatives from all over the Empire; their trade-marks are preserved in the mosaic flooring.

Passing one of the finest private houses in the city, the House of Apuleius with its peristyle and atrium, the route now leads on to the **Mithraeum** [J]; the symbols of the ancient cult of Mithras can still be seen on the walls of the temple. Next come the **Horrea** [K], 64 warehouses for the storage of corn, opposite the **Collegium Augustale** [L]. On the Via dei Molini, which runs the length of the Horrea, is the **Casa di Diana** [M] with an unusual projecting balcony. The fascinating **Casa dei Dipinti**, an ancient apartment-house, lies on the way to the museum containing the best finds from the excavations. Back on the main road, we now arrive at the **Forum** [N] with the remains of the majestic *Capitolium* (early 2nd-century AD), and opposite it the remains of the Temple of Rome and Augustus (1st century AD). At the **Curia** [O], or Senate House – with lists of citizens on its walls – and the **Tempio Rotondo** [P], erected to the worship of the emperors, the Decumano Massimo makes a turn.

The Forum

A Classical pose

We now pass the **Macellum** [Q], or market; the **Terme dalle sei Colonne** [R]; the **Schola di Traiano** [S], a restored house with a peristyle; and on the other side of the road a two-aisled Christian **basilica** [T], which must originally have formed part of the baths. The Via della Foce that branches off here leads to the **Terme dei Sette Sapienti** [U], baths with a round central hall, paved with a mosaic showing hunting motifs. The **Insula del Serapide** [V] and the **Insula degli Aurighi** [W] are good examples of Roman apartment blocks; a stairway leading up to a second floor has been preserved. The **Case a Giardino** [X], four blocks built in the 2nd century AD, once surrounded a magnificent garden. There are fine frescoes and mosaics in the Casa dalle Volte Dipinti and the Insula delle Muse.

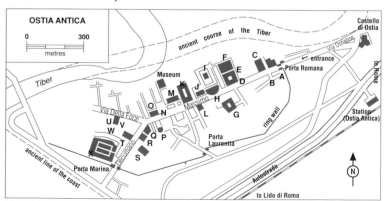

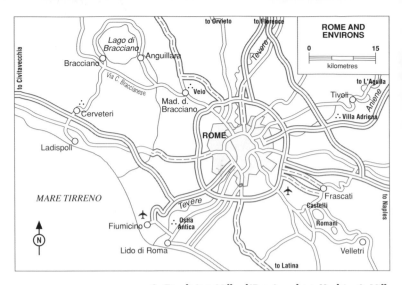

2. Tivoli (★★ Villa d'Este) and ★★ Hadrian's Villa

The small town of Tivoli lies in the Sabine Hills roughly 32km (20 miles) from Rome. It can be reached by car along the Via Tiburtina; by train along the Rome–Pescara line; and also by buses that leave half-hourly from the Via Gaeta near the Piazza dei Cinquecento (Stazione Termini). Tivoli, famed for its fountains and springs, has been a popular health resort ever since antiquity.

Entrance, Villa d'Este

16th-century frescoes, Villa d'Este

★★ **Villa d'Este** (open daily except Monday 9.30am–dusk): in the summer months it is illuminated in the evenings until around midnight. Built on the ruins of a Roman villa, the Villa d'Este was constructed in 1550 by the Cardinal d'Este as a summer palazzo. The apartments, with their **16th-century frescoes** of the Roman school, are definitely worth visiting; Franz Liszt lived here from 1865 to the year of his death, and it was here that he wrote his popular piano piece *Les Jeux d'eaux à la Villa d'Este*. The gardens, with their fountains, are among the loveliest in Italy.

Starting from the palace, begin your stroll at the Grotto of Diana, with its stuccoes on mythological themes. A little further on is the semicircular terrace known as Rometta (Little Rome), a miniature of the city with the island in the Tiber and small-scale reproductions of the main monuments.

Opposite the Rometta is the Viale delle Cento Fontane, which leads right across the garden, ending up at the Fontane dell'Ovato (Oval Fountain). The statues of nymphs are by Giovanni Battista Della Porta. A path leads away from this fountain to the Fontana dell'Organo Idraulico, with its statues of Orpheus and Apollo. The water-operated organ designed by the Frenchman Claude Venard was considered one of the wonders of the 16th century. Opposite, three fishponds come into view. The path after the first of them leads across to the right to the Rotonda dei Cipressi, with some of the mightiest cypresses in Italy. In the opposite direction is the Fontana dei Draghi (Dragon Fountain), erected in 1572, recalling the dragons in the coat-of-arms of Gregory XIII. If you keep to the right here you will reach the Rometta again.

Roman remains, Tivoli

★★ **Hadrian's Villa** (open daily except Monday 9am–dusk). Hadrian's Villa lies on the Via Tiburtina outside Tivoli, and there is a regular bus service.

The emperor Hadrian had the villa built in the 2nd century AD; many of the buildings here take their inspiration from famous classical monuments that had impressed Hadrian on his many travels through the Empire. A pavilion at the carpark contains a reconstruction of the entire complex, giving an idea of the sheer size of the largest and richest imperial villa.

Caryatids on the canal, Tivoli

The works of art discovered here have all found their way into the museums of Rome and the Vatican. Sights worth seeing include the restored Teatro Marittimo (Maritime Theatre); the celebrated *Canopus*, designed to imitate the famous sanctuary of Serapis near Alexandria; the Major Baths; and the Greek Theatre.

79

3. ★ *Lago di Bracciano*

The Lago di Bracciano, a lake northwest of Rome, is an anglers' and swimmers' paradise. There is a bus connection from the Metro station of Lepanto. Motorists should leave Rome along the Via Cassia and travel to Madonna di Bracciano (17km/10½ miles from Rome); a 5km (3 mile) detour leads to the ruins of ★ **Veio** (one of the most famous of the Etruscan cities, built between the 8th and 6th century BC).

Travel further along the Via Braccianese, then turn off it to the fishing village of Anguillara (Sabazia), 38km (24 miles) from Rome and right next to the lake. The Lago di Bracciano is of volcanic origin – it was once a crater. In the town of Bracciano is the ★ **Castello Orsini-Odescalchi**, a superbly-preserved Renaissance baronial castle, built by the Orsini family in the late 15th century.

A trip to Cerveteri and the Etruscan ★ **necropolis** there is a very worthwhile detour. All the various methods of burial are represented here in the fenced-in *zona monumentale*; there are literally hundreds of tombs (open in summer Tuesday to Saturday 9am–dusk, Sunday 10am–dusk; in winter Tuesday to Saturday 9am–4pm, Sunday 10am–4pm).

Art History

Early history

Early settlement of Roman territory during the Middle and Late Bronze Ages (16th–10th century BC) was mainly by shepherds, as evidenced by various burial objects (vases and terracottas). The Iron Age (9th century BC onwards) is better documented, especially by the archaic *Sepolcre-tum* (necropolis) of the Forum Romanum (*see page 26*): funeral urns shaped like the huts of that time contained burial objects representing miniature versions of daily household implements. Parallel to this a cultural exchange between north and south began to develop, between Etruria and the Greek colonies in Southern Italy. This is also evidenced by finds made around the cemetery, which was shifted to the Esquiline when the town started to expand. Vases of Etruscan and Greek origin, terracotta figurines and bronze implements reveal a high level of knowledge and prosperity.

Letters in stone, Forum Romanum

Foreign influences

The period of Etruscan rule brought the Romans the alphabet (which the Etruscans had borrowed from the Greeks), and certain Hellenic art-forms; indeed, later Roman art would have been unthinkable without Greek and Etruscan influence. The Etruscan architect Vulca built a Capitoline temple to Jupiter, Juno and Minerva in 509BC. The first marble temple was built by the Greek architect Hermodoros – at a time when Rome already controlled the entire Mediterranean. In the year 335BC, after the young Republic had achieved a degree of stability both internally and externally, it began minting coins, also on the Greek model. This ushered in a renewed phase of prosperity for Rome. The city's expansionist policies automatically resulted in the transfer of artistic works from conquered territories to the new metropolis – hundreds of wagons and ships brought thousands of statues, sculptures and other priceless artistic treasures to Rome. These trophies soon became sought-after status symbols for the city's upper classes. Demand for Greek sculpture could be successfully quelled only by producing a series of high-quality copies; indeed, we have Roman copiers to thank for the fact that so many of the most important works of Greek classical sculpture have survived to this day. Deprived of their original cult function the sculptures epitomised a cultural ideal which the Romans also strove to emulate in their own artistic endeavours.

Capitoline Venus

The influence of Greek art

The Roman conquest between 212BC and 30BC of *Magna Graecia* (Greater Greece, ie Southern Italy), of the Greek motherland and of the Hellenistic Empire in Asia Minor and Africa also resulted in the emigration of many Greek artists to Rome. Under their influence, Roman architecture and sculpture flourished and attained new heights of artistic perfection. The tendency – already observable in Hellenism – towards the gradual individualisation of the human form was reflected in Roman art's need for prestige. Individual portraiture also seems to have had an influence: the deceased were often portrayed as full sculptures lying on their sarcophagi. Roman portrait busts were also part of the politically motivated artistic programme that lent visual emphasis to the rhetoric of the rulers. They were supplemented by low-relief, continuous narrative sculpture on triumphal arches and columns, depicting historical scenes and glorifying the exploits of generals and emperors. This form of sculpture, too, had its antecedents in Greek art; the latter, however, have survived only in pictorial form (wall paintings of the Battle of Marathon, Delphi).

Bust of philosopher, Capitoline Museums

Roman architecture

In architecture, Roman independence was expressed by an abandonment of three-dimensionality in external design. The Greek temple with its pillars and low stylobate was not copied. Rome tended to adopt the podium of the Etruscan temple, with a flight of steps on the entrance facade. The rear wall remained unemphasised, and the axial character of the whole was accentuated by a pillared atrium. The axial symmetry and facade orientation of Roman buildings allowed new city-planning solutions to be achieved which were to remain the rule for the post-

Temple of Hercules

Antique world as well. The revolutionary architectural form of the basilica (hall of justice and commerce) was one of the most significant successes of Roman architecture; others included such achievements of the imperial era as the circus, theatre, amphitheatre, round temple and baths.

Rome's own individual principles of construction and decoration were all at the forefront here: ornamental forms and applied columns; arches, barrel and groined barrel vaults, domed structures and buttresses; imperial busts, triumphal arches and reliefs; sarcophagi and statues, but above all facade design. The new secular structures were astonishingly well planned: palaces, villas, baths, theatres, aqueducts, bridges, and legal and commercial centres (basilicas). During the *pax romana* the ruling class celebrated its need for prestige through the creation of mosaics, sculpture and painting.

Trajan's markets

Painting and mosaics

Roman floor mosaic

It was painting which reached the highest levels of development, though in Rome very few traces of it remain. It was the important finds in Pompeii that really made this Roman art famous. It was discovered that the painters of antiquity already knew all about portrait-painting, still-life, genre painting, monumental painting and perspective painting – achievements that were only regained in Western painting in around the year 1300.

This ancient art vanished along with the Roman Empire, especially because early Christianity stood in theological opposition to the profanity of pagan art and of pictorial representation in general.

The highly-developed art of mosaics was adopted by the young church for purely ritual reasons. For centuries, its iconic style remained incompatible with any subjective rendition of form. Despite its iconoclastic leanings, the doctrine of Christianity advocated the evidential value of pictorial representation in the face of popular illiteracy. Adaptation of the widespread symbolic language used in the Roman mystic cult of Mithras was meant to facilitate the transfer of popular belief to the Christian religion.

Pagan and Early Christian paintings are often hard to tell apart, just like the Christian and non-Christian tombs alongside each other in the catacombs. The fact that the pictorial language already inherent in Christianity was open to so many different interpretations provided the religion with one of its best chances of survival. The oldest Christian paintings date from the 2nd century AD (Catacombs of Priscilla), though most of them are 3rd- and 4th-century; and the cult of the Virgin Mary was first introduced to the religion in the 5th century at the Council of Ephesus (431).

Early Christian architecture

The Edict of Milan in 313 paved the way for a Christian architectural style. The first building to be erected was San Giovanni in Laterano (St John Lateran), then came Old St Peter's, consecrated to the first pope, and the original building of San Paolo fuori le Mura (St Paul's Outside the Walls) for the Apostle Paul. Since the Early Christian type of sacred building was out of the question here (the centralised structure was only used for baptisteries), the secular form of the Roman basilica was used: an axial, multi-aisled hall with windows piercing the high walls, and with the centre aisle built higher and broader than those at either side.

The semicircular protrusion on the narrow side, where Roman dignitaries formerly sat, became the apse, and an atrium was placed in front of the entrance hall. The altar finally ended up at the intersection of apse and nave; the crypt containing the saints' holy relics lay beneath the altar in both St Peter's and St Paul's. After attending liturgy, the faithful then went to the holy tomb in a procession in order to touch it, and since Old St Peter's could hold a congregation of 14,000 the steps leading down to the crypt had to be widened considerably.

For this very practical reason, additional structures became necessary to the left and right of the altar; these became the transepts, which accidentally went on to form the cross shape; the latter became the decisive and exemplary ground-plan for all churches, even where broad flights of steps to accommodate processions were quite unnecessary.

Medieval times (c 500 onwards)

The transfer of the seat of power to Constantinople in the year 330, the division of the Empire into an eastern and a western part in 395 and the demise of the West Roman Empire in 476 weakened Rome's leading role considerably. The centuries of tribal incursion and the hegemony of the peoples north of the Alps also resulted in a marked decline in Rome's artistic importance.

Rome's attractions for pilgrims (above all its martyrs' tombs and the papacy) meant that it was still in touch with at least a few of the artistic developments that were taking place elsewhere: Romanesque art, for instance, left strong traces on the city, and Byzantine mosaics achieved new heights of magnificence in the city's churches between the 9th and 13th centuries. Rome actually possesses only one Gothic church, Santa Maria sopra Minerva (*see page 22*). This was due to the decline of the city, which literally became deserted after the transferral of the seat of the papacy to Avignon (1309–77) and the western schism (1378 onwards).

Byzantine mosaic, San Clemente

Renaissance (late 15th century onwards)

An entire millennium had passed Rome by before its papacy again became strong enough to form the basis for the city's renewed ascendancy during the Renaissance (and later also the baroque) period. Under Pope Nicholas V (1447–55) and his art-loving successors, Rome flourished culturally and artistically as the centre of Christianity. Emancipation from church doctrine and a growing historical awareness brought the glorious legacy of antiquity to the fore.

This Renaissance, or rebirth, of the culture of antiquity spread to include all forms of art. The dome and portico of the Pantheon became the model for countless other variations on the same theme. At the end of the 15th century Rome became a city of Renaissance masterpieces.

The facades of Sant'Agostino dei Portoghesi (*see page 75*) and Santa Maria del Popolo (*see page 70*) are fine examples of Early Renaissance church architecture, and the Palazzo Venezia (*see page 16*) of the palace architecture of that time. The High Renaissance is best illustrated by the Sistine Chapel (*see page 65*), the Tempietto in the courtyard of San Pietro in Montorio (*see page 68*), the Palazzo della Cancelleria and the Palazzo Farnese (*see page 19*). The most important artists during this period were Bramante (1444–1514), Michelangelo (1475–1564) and Raphael (1483–1520). All three received commissions from the architecturally ambitious pope Julius II (1503–13); all three were involved in the building of St Peter's (*see page 53*); and all three were far more than just architects. Michelangelo, who built the dome of St Peter's,

Palazzo della Cancelleria

Sistine Chapel

is just as famous as a sculptor (*Pietà* in St Peter's, *Moses* in San Pietro in Vincoli) and especially as a painter (Sistine Chapel); and Raphael, who decorated a large papal apartment in the Vatican single-handed, the Stanza della Segnatura, is, of course, a painter of world renown. Today the Via Giulia (*see page 19*), one of the city's large, straight traffic arteries, stands in memory of both Michelangelo and Raphael – an expression of Renaissance antiquity in medieval Rome that also marks the beginning of modern city planning.

Baroque (late 16th century onwards)

The geometrical severity and precision of triangles and right-angles that is such a characteristic of Renaissance architecture disappeared entirely in Roman baroque, which set a precedent for the style throughout Europe in general. The transition between the two styles is well illustrated by the facade of Santa Caterina dei Funari, which was built between 1560 and 1564; the severity of its Renaissance contours is slightly tempered by the odd curve, clearly presaging the baroque.

Bernini colonnade

However, the real prototype for countless baroque structures was the facade of the Gesù (*see page 18*), which dates from 1575. Here, Early baroque has still not entirely dispensed with the right-angle and with geometrical precision; this only took place during the high baroque period, fine examples being the consistently designed Chiesa Nuova and the Oratorio dei Filippini (*see page 20*). St Peter's Square by Lorenzo Bernini (*see page 53*) and his angels in Sant'Andrea delle Fratte show the baroque style 'in full swing'; the unique Piazza Navona with Bernini's fountains (*see page 21*) and the facade of Sant'Agnese in Agone enchant every visitor to the city.

Fontana dei Quattro Fiumi

Bernini's rival, Francesco Borromini, provided his own unique additions to the exuberance of Roman baroque. His fluid and active convex and concave masses and surfaces seem almost to defy gravity, and he denied the restrictive, enclosing qualities of walls in order to treat space and light as architectonic components. Borromini's real masterpiece is San Carlo alle Quattro Fontane (*see page 43*); a century passed before its revolutionary baroque forms were adopted at the beginning of the 18th century by South German baroque architects. This dissolution of form was also a major feature of baroque painting. Ceilings of baroque churches dissolved in painted scenes with foreshortening, presenting vivid views of the infinite to the worshipper (Il Gesù, *see page 18*), and illusionistic architecture and decoration predominated alongside a healthy naturalism. The main exponents among a whole host of artists were Caravaggio (1560–1609) and Domenichino (1581–1641).

Neoclassicism (late 18th century onwards)

In direct contrast to the baroque style, neoclassicism once again made use of Renaissance and antique elements, dispensing with useless ornamentation. The simplicity and grandeur of antique art became the yardstick of neoclassicism, with its heroic sobriety. The architecture of the Vatican Museums accurately expresses their scientific orientation. The neoclassicism of this period included the fantastic documentary etchings of Piranesi, the paintings by the German Romantics who had chosen to live in Rome, and the 'euphoric' archaeology of Winckelmann. Under Napoleon's influence Roman neoclassicism finally received its imperialist edge, so evident in the layout of the Piazza del Popolo and of the Pincio.

Bracio Nuovo, Chiaramonti Gallery, Vatican

20th century

The enormous Monumento Nazionale a Vittorio Emanuele II that was built at the turn of the century throws even the Capitoline Hill itself out of scale. This controversial structure is familiarly known as 'the Wedding Cake'. Other buildings dating from the same period, which was marked by rapid industrial expansion, include the monumental Palazzo di Giustizia next to the Castel Sant'Angelo, the Palazzo delle Esposizioni on the Via Nazionale, and also the Garibaldi statue on the Gianicolo (Janiculum). Another spate of feverish building activity between the two wars, during the two decades of Italian Fascism, altered the face of the city still further: on the right bank of the Tiber, at the foot of Monte Mario, the Foro Italico was constructed; its Stadio dei Marmi (Marble Stadium) was decorated with 60 colossal statues of athletes. Construction work also began on the new railway station building (Stazione Termini), though it was finally completed only in 1950.

Rome would have hosted a World Exhibition in 1942 had it not been for World War II; however, some building work had already begun in preparation for it along the city's southern edge. This new quarter was known as EUR (the letters stand for Esposizione Universale di Roma), and after the war it became a modern residential area with its own administrative buildings, sports facilities and museums (including the Museo delle Arti e delle Tradizione Popolari, the Museo Preistorico ed Etnografico and also the Museo della Civiltà Romana, which illustrates the history of Rome and its cultural achievements). The choice of Rome to host the Olympic Summer Games in 1960 provided the city with a whole series of sports facilities: the Palazzo dello Sport (in the EUR), the Stadio Flaminio and the Palazzetto dello Sport (on the Via Flaminia), and the Stadio Olimpico in the Foro Italico. These structures form an interesting link between modern sports architecture and that of imperial Rome (*see page 7*).

Garibaldi monument

Music and Theatre

Classical

Rome can be justly proud of its classical concerts, given the range of atmospheric venues, from concert halls to churches, from Renaissance piazzas to Roman amphitheatres. The concert season runs from October to June.

First-rate concerts are put on by the **Accademia Nazionale di Santa Cecilia**, Auditorium di Santa Cecilia, Via della Conciliazione 4 (near St Peter's Square and Castel Sant'Angelo). Santa Cecilia is the city's top symphony orchestra. The box office is at Via Vittoria 6 (near the Spanish Steps), tel: 654 10 44 or 678 07 42. In summer, the Santa Cecilia orchestra also performs in churches, or outdoors, especially in the grounds of Villa Giulia.

Orchestra Sinfonica della RAI, the orchestra of the RAI, the state broadcasting network, presents a series of Saturday evening concerts in the Auditorio del Foro Italico, Piazza Lauro de Bosis 5, tel: 36 86 56 25.

Classical concert venues: Chamber music and recitals are often staged in Teatro Olimpico, Piazza Gentile da Fabriano 17, tel: 323 49 08 or 323 49 36. Other popular venues for classical concerts are Castel Sant'Angelo, Palazzo della Cancelleria, and the Basilica di Massenzio.

Summer concert venues: Open-air summer concerts are staged in Piazza del Campidoglio (Capitoline Hill). In addition, check posters and *TrovaRoma, La Repubblica*'s Thursday supplement, for details of summer festivals and concerts held in churches, parks or villas.

Out on the town

Rock, Jazz and Folk Music

Rome is a popular stop on the European rock circuit and most international touring bands will play in the city. Native Roman bands show little innovation on the rock front but the city has a lively jazz scene, helped by the publicity generated by the annual Roma Jazz Festival. Certain Jazz, Latin and World Music clubs, particularly those situated in the Trastevere and Testaccio quarters, attract a devoted following. Check details in the "Music Box" section of *TrovaRoma, La Repubblica*'s Thursday supplement.

Opera

Rome's Teatro dell'Opera may be among Italy's top five opera companies, but can't compete with Milan's La Scala or Naples' San Carlo. Instead, the Roman opera company plays safe, with a classical repertoire and a focus on broad-canvas drama and a Roman love of spectacle.

The opera season runs from November to May and is based on the company of Teatro dell'Opera, which usually performs in Piazza Beniamino Gigli (off Via Viminale). Tel: 481 70 03 or 48 16 01. In summer (July and

August) marvellous open-air performances take place in the Baths of Caracalla (Terme di Caracalla), Viale delle Terme di Caracalla 52. *Aida*, staged with live elephants, is popular with the crowds. Tickets can be booked at the Teatro dell'Opera box office or bought at the entrance.

Ballet and dance are not very well-represented in Rome but, from the point of view of spectacle, at least, take the opportunity to see a summer ballet performed at the Baths of Caracalla.

Theatre

Roman theatre embraces mainstream and contemporary theatre but the emphasis is on the tried and trusted Italian dramatists, such as Carlo Goldoni and Luigi Pirandello. However, the university theatres and smaller venues do stage fringe productions. The theatre season runs from October to early June but there are numerous summer events that are linked to specific Roman festivals.

Mainstream Theatre Venues:

Teatro Argentina, Largo Argentina 56, tel: 68 80 46 01.
Teatro Eliseo, Via Nazionale 183, tel: 488 21 14.
Teatro Piccolo Eliseo, Via Nazionale 183, tel: 48 85 95.
Teatro Sistina, Via Sistina 129, tel: 482 68 41.

Contemporary or Experimental Theatre Venues:

Teatro Ateneo, Viale delle Scienze 3, tel: 49 91 44 35. (Rome University theatre.)
Teatro Colosseo, Via Capo d'Africa 5A, tel: 700 49 32. Experimental or fringe theatre.
Teatro Tordinona, Via degli Acquasparta 16, tel: 68 80 58 90. (Rome University theatre.)

Puppet Theatre and Cabaret Venues:

Ciceruacchio, Via del Porto 1, tel: 580 60 46. Traditional Roman cabaret restaurant in Trastevere.
English Puppet Theatre, Via di Grotta Pinta 2, tel: 589 62 01. Performances of puppet shows in English.
Teatro Mongiovino, Via Genocchi 15, tel: 513 94 05. Traditional puppet theatre in Italian.

Summer Spectacle

Anfiteatro Quercia del Tasso, Passeggiata del Gianicolo (Janiculum Hill), Viale Aldo Fabrizi, tel: 575 08 27. Summer open-air performances of theatre and dance in the amphitheatre.

Teatro Romano di Ostia Antica, Viale dei Romagnoli 717, Ostia Antica, tel: 565 00 22 or 565 14 05. Outdoor theatrical performances in the Roman theatre.

Teatro Villa Adriana, Tivoli, tel: 65 44 601. Outdoor performances in Hadrian's Villa at Tivoli.

Theatre

Food and Drink

Opposite: an inviting shop window

Rome provides a huge and colourful selection of places to eat out. The city is also considerably cheaper than Milan, Florence or Venice. As elsewhere in Italy, meals usually consist of three courses: *primo piatto* (first course), *secondo* (second) and dessert; side-dishes *(contorni)* usually need to be ordered and paid for separately. Those not desperately keen to sample great-name wines can safely stick to *vino sfuso* (regional house wine served from the carafe). Like all other major Italian cities, Rome has a whole series of self-service restaurants, often called *Rosticceria, Tavola Calda, Self-Service, Fast-Food,* etc.

Pasta

Pizzerias serve every variation straight from the oven. Romans adore pizza, and usually accompany it with beer. Some former milk shops, still known as *latterie*, have a few tables laid out where delicious home-made cakes can be sampled. The same applies to former wine bars and vintners' shops, still known as *vinaio* or *bottigleria*. The Romans have a special version of the ubiquitous *trattoria*: the *hostaria*, an old-fashioned word for the more familiar *osteria*. These restaurants serve local specialities that are often of very high quality. And the *pasticceria* should also be mentioned; it is a cake shop where drinks are often served at a small bar to accompany home-made cakes and pastries.

91

Rome actually has no typical restaurant area. The historic centre between the Tiber and the Via del Corso is a good place for culinary explorations, as is the picturesque quarter of Trastevere.

Roman specialities

Many dishes with the suffix *alla romana* have become internationally famous: *saltimbocca alla romana* is a delicious schnitzel filled with ham and cheese and rounded off with a dash of sage; *trippa alla romana* (tripe) is a typical example of Roman *cucina povera* (poor man's cuisine). *Zuppa romana* comes in several versions, but is basically a trifle with candied fruit that should officially be drenched in rum. The Romans are particularly ambitious when it comes to pasta dishes, and the sauces that go with them aren't always traditionally based on tomatoes: there are several very interesting variations of spaghetti sauce under the heading of *pasta in bianco*, which get by without any tomato at all.

Waiter

By the way, spaghetti should only be eaten as an hors d'oeuvre, not as a main dish. As elsewhere in Italy, fish plays an important role in the cuisine. The following are particularly recommended: *anguilla al lauro* (eel with laurel), *triglie al forno* (baked red mullet) and *branzino in bianco* (steamed sea bass).

A cappuccino

A famous establishment

Restaurants
$$$ expensive, $$ reasonable, $ cheap.

Piazza del Popolo, Spanish Steps, Via Veneto
Alfredo All'Augusto L'Originale, Piazza Augusto Imperatore, tel: 687 8615. Known for its *fettucine*. $$

Andrea, Via Sardegna 26, tel: 493707. Rich ingredients and traditional menus. Excellent pasta dishes. $$$

Colline Emiliane, Via degli Avignonesi 22, tel: 481 7538. Friendly, family-run *trattoria*. $$

La Cupola dell' Hotel Excelsior, Via Veneto 125, tel: 396 4708. International dishes. $$$

Piazza Navona, Pantheon, Campo de' Fiori, Ghetto
Al Pompiere, Via Santa Maria dei Calderai 38, tel: 686 8377. Refined Roman cooking in an old palazzo. $$

Giggetto, Via del Portico d'Ottavia 21, tel: 686 1105. Well-known *trattoria* in the ghetto. $$

Il Drappo, Vicolo del Malpasso, tel: 687 7 365. Serves Sardinian specialities and Sardinian wines. $$

Papa Giovanni, Via dei Sediari 4, tel: 686 5308. The accent is on the use of seasonal foods. $$$

Porto di Ripetta, Via di Ripetta 250, tel: 361 2376. Specialities include seafood dishes. $$

Trattoria Fortunato, Via del Pantheon 55, tel: 679 2788. Refined Roman cuisine, fresh fish. $$$

Trastevere
Alberto Ciarla, Piazza S. Cosimato 40, tel: 581 8668. Famous for its fish dishes (and fish tank). $$$

Cul de Sac 2, Vicolo dell'Atleta 21, tel: 581 3324. An elegant and innovative restaurant. $$$

Stazione Termini, Via Nazionale, Colosseo
Ai Tre Scalini, Rossana e Matteo, Via di Santi Quatro 30, tel: 70 96 309. Menu includes *couscous*. $$

Taverna dei 40, Via Claudia 24, tel: 736296. Genuine old-fashioned Roman *osteria*. $

Testaccio
Checchino dal 1887, Via Monte Testaccio 30, tel: 574 6318. Excellently prepared Roman cuisine. $$$

Turiddu al Mattatoio, Viale Galvani 64, tel: 575 0447. Family *trattoria*, typical Roman cuisine. $

Outside the centre
Loreto, Via Valenziani 19, tel: 736276. Particularly good fish dishes. In the direction of Villa Torlonia. $$$

Relais Le Jardin dell' Hotel Lord Byron, Via Giuseppe De Notaris 5, tel: 322 0404. Housed in a former monastery, one of the best restaurants in Italy. $$$

Shopping

What to buy

Rome is the place for quality rather than bargains so its best buys tend to be almost exclusively at the luxury end of the market. That said, careful shoppers may still come away with attractive books on art and architecture, striking kitchenware, herbalists' concoctions, distinctive marbled notepaper from a cartoleria, a stylish modern lamp, or an appealing old print. Regional wines, cheeses and olive oil also represent good value.

However, the city really comes into its own with leather and designer goods. Attractive purchases include leatherware, designer luggage, ceramics, elegant or rustic glassware, designer lighting, inlaid marble tables, gold jewellery and objets d'art. There is also no shortage of antiques and hand-crafted furniture.

Antiques

The main shopping areas are the **Via del Corso** and the streets branching off it towards the Spanish Steps, with their equally elegant shops and equally elegant customers. Popular shopping streets include the **Via del Tritone**, the **Via Nazionale** and the **Via Cola di Rienzo**.

Markets

Markets are the places to go to experience the nitty gritty of Roman life.

Campo de' Fiori, Piazza Campo de' Fiori. This is the liveliest and most colourful fruit and vegetable market. There are also several flower stalls, good delicatessens and bars around the square. Monday Saturday, 6am–2pm.

Mercato dei Fiori, Via Trionfale (Prati).The covered wholesale flower market sells the whole range of Mediterranean plants and flowers. Tuesday 10am–1pm.

Mercato di San Cosimato, Piazza di San Cosimato, Trastevere. This small, popular fruit and vegetable market is set in an attractive square. Weekday mornings.

Mercato di Via Sannio, Piazza San Giovanni in Laterano quarter (San Giovanni metro stop). A clothes market that also sells vintage and second-hand designer clothes in stalls abutting the Aurelian Walls. Monday to Friday 7.30am–1pm, Saturday 7.30am–6pm.

Mercato delle Stampe (or Mercato di Fontanelle Borghese, Largo della Fontanelle Borghese). Sells prints and second-hand or antiquarian books. Monday to Saturday 7am–1pm.

Porta Portese, Via Portuense and Via Ippolito Nievo, Trastevere. The best flea market in Rome. Awaiting your delectation are reproduction antiques, Mussolini memorabilia, Russian military insignia, cast-off clothes and jewellery, pirated cassettes, kitchen equipment, caviare and icons, plants and pets. Sunday 6.30am–2pm.

Market stall

Getting There

Opposite: one of Rome's few remaining trams

By air

There are several flights a day from London to Rome, with both British Airways and the national airline Alitalia; Alitalia also operates daily direct flights from New York and other cities in the US. The major carriers all offer special fares of varying types; it's best to ring the individual airline. During the holiday season, Rome is also a popular destination for charter flights. Rome's Leonardo da Vinci airport is situated in Fiumicino near Ostia, 35km (22 miles) away from the centre. There are direct train connections to Ostiense Station every 20 minutes, and the trip costs around 6,000 lire. From there, buses or Metro trains connect with every part of the city.

By rail

There are daily connections to Rome from most major European cities. Services within Italy itself vary a great deal in both speed and comfort, from the *Locale* trains which stop at every station to the *Pendolino*, the luxurious high-speed train that runs between Rome and Milan, Genoa, Turin, Venice, Bari and Naples. Operating between Rome, Venice, Milan, Florence and Naples, Intercity trains have both first- and second-class carriages; prior booking is recommended during the high season.

Night trains have a sleeper/couchette service. Information about reductions and special fares available from ticket offices, travel agents and other sales agencies. In Rome: information at the main station, Stazione Termini.

By car

From whichever direction you arrive, you will always land up on the *Grande Raccordo Anulare*, or GRA, Rome's equivalent of the M25. The main streets to the centre lead off it like the spokes of a wheel.

A driving licence and vehicle registration documents, a warning triangle and country stickers are compulsory. The international green insurance card doesn't have to be shown at the border but is advisable in case of accident; comprehensive cover is recommended.

The maximum speed allowed on Italy's toll motorways is 130kmph (80mph) for cars with capacities of over 1.1 litres; smaller vehicles may not travel faster than 110kmph (68mph); and the usual limit on country roads is 90kmph (56mph). Seat belts have been compulsory in Italy since 1989. Petrol in Italy is extremely expensive.

In case of breakdown tel:116, emergencies tel: 113. Members of automobile associations can get help from the ACI (Italian Automobile Club): Via Marsala 8, I-00185 Roma, tel: 49981.

Little Fiats, designed for narrow streets

Leave the car behind

Getting Around

Parking

Rome is not an easy city to drive in: there are almost no parking-spaces available anywhere. To reduce the amount of traffic, the historic centre is closed to cars on weekdays from 7–11am and from 3–7pm.

Parking is outside the pedestrian precincts; there are multi-storeys below the Villa Borghese (access from the Porta Pinciana) and in the Parking Ludovisi (access via the Via Veneto and the Via Ludovisi which branches off it). Only park in supervised carparks – it is a false economy to do otherwise.

Get a map for the buses

Buses

It is advisable to get a bus map *(Roma in Metro-Bus)* on arrival in Rome; they are available from the kiosk at the bus station in the Piazza dei Cinquecento (in front of the main railway station, Stazione Termini), and also from international newsstands.

Bus tickets (800 lire) can be bought from ATAC ticket offices at the respective termini, at major line intersections such as Largo Argentina or Piazzale Flaminio, or at tobacconists and newsagents.

The bus map provides information (also in English) about operating times, night buses, ticket prices and various discount fares such as the tourist weekly ticket. Special day tickets allowing unlimited travel (also on Metro trains) cost 2,800 lire.

Metro

Rome's Metro stations (short for *Metropolitana*) are marked by a large red 'M'; the two lines A and B meet up at the main station (Stazione Termini). The respective routes are:

Line A: Anagnina – Cinecittà – Colli Albani – San Giovanni in Laterano – Termini – Piazza della Repubblica – Piazza Barberini – Piazza di Spagna – Piazzale Flaminio – Lepanto – Ottaviano.

Line B: Termini – Via Cavour – Colosseo – Circo Massimo – Porta San Paolo (Piramide) – Basilica di S Paolo – EUR – Laurentina.

Ostia Antica and Ostia Lido lines: direct trains *(treni)* depart every 30 minutes from the Porta San Paolo (Piramide) as well as from the Termini and Magliana Metro stations.

Motor Ship Tiber 1

Between April and October this ship does daily trips from the Porta Portese to Ostia Antica (ticket also includes guided tour of Ostia Antica). Information from Tourvisa Italia, Via Marghera 32 (near the main station), tel: 493481.

Trams

Rome's few remaining trams are mostly to be found in the suburbs; one particularly delightful round trip can be made on the tram line No 30 described in *Route 8, A tram ride around Rome* (*see page 67*).

This is the way the Italians ride

Taxis

These can either be hired at cab-ranks in the city centre or ordered by phone (tel: 3570, 3875, 4994). There are no cruising taxis. Be sure to negotiate the fare first, especially for longer journeys.

No-cruising cabs

Hire cars

All the major car-hire companies have outlets in Rome, and usually have special weekend rates or unlimited mileage deals; further information either from hotels or directly from the firms themselves.

City round trips

Three major travel agencies organise half-day-long and all-day-long city round trips, and also a Rome By Night tour: CIT, Piazza della Repubblica 68; American Express, Piazza Mignanelli; Univers, Galleria Filippo Caracciolo 20a. The city round trips organised by the municipal transport authority ATAC are also recommended; departures daily from the Piazza Cinquecento (Stazione Termini), from 3.30pm.

Bicycles

If you're feeling adventurous, discovering Rome by bike is an experience not to be missed. There are cycle-hire outlets (Coop Bici-Roma) in the Old City at the Salita dei Crescenzi (Pantheon), Piazza del Popolo, Piazza Augusto Imperatore, Largo dei Lombardi, Piazza Sonnino and Piazza Navona; another possibility is the firm Collalti, Via del Pellegrino 82.

Facts for the Visitor

Travel documents

Visitors from the US, EU and Commonwealth countries need only a passport for a stay of up to three months; a visa is not required. Citizens of other countries should check with the nearest Italian consultate about obtaining a visa in advance of travel.

Customs

You're allowed to bring in as much currency as you like. Non-EU members can bring 400 cigarettes, one bottle of spirits, two of wine and 50g of perfume; EU-members have guide levels of 800 cigarettes, 10 litres of spirit and 90 litres of wine. Customs keep a close watch for drugs, which are illegal.

Currency Regulations

There is no limit on the amount of lire that can be taken into or out of the country, although for cash transactions there is a restriction of 20 million lire. This also applies within Italy itself.

Information

Information can be obtained from the offices of the Italian State Tourist Office (ENIT) at the following addresses:

In the UK: Italian State Tourist Office, 1 Princes Street, London W1, tel: 0171-408 1254; fax: 0171-493 6695.

In the US: Italian Government Tourist Office, 630 5th Avenue, Suite 1565, NY 10111, New York, tel: 212 245 4822; fax: 212 586 9249.

In Rome: I-80100 Roma, Via Marghera 2, tel: 4971282. There is also a branch of ENIT at Leonardo da Vinci airport (Fiumicino).

EPT (Provincial Tourist Office), I-80185 Roma, Via Parigi 11, tel: 4881851/5 and Via Parigi 5, tel: 4883748; also at the main station (Stazione Termini), on the A1 (autostrada Roma–Milano), A2 (autostrada Roma–Napoli) and at Leonardo da Vinci airport.

Carta Giovani (Young person's pass)

Young people between 16 and 26 years of age can obtain this pass free of charge at information bureaux. It provides several discounts. Don't forget to bring with you a passport-sized photo plus passport.

Banca Italia

Money

The basic unit of currency is the *lira*, plural *lire* (L). Coins are issued in denominations of 50, 100, 200 and 500 lire; banknotes in 1,000, 2,000, 10,000, 20,000 50,000 and 100,000 lire.

Banks and Exchange

Banks are open Monday to Friday 8.30am–1pm and 2.45–3.45pm. Currency exchange outlets (including Stazione Termini) are open longer, also at weekends and on public holidays.

Traveller's cheques and cheques can be changed at most hotels. Eurocheques are accepted to a value of 300,000 lire, and up to 1 million lire can be withdrawn from post office savings accounts.

Bank rates vary but are usually the most favourable. *Bureaux de change* charge a commission for each transaction, however small the amount.

Bureau de change

Bills

Restaurants and other establishments are now required by law (for tax reasons) to issue an official receipt to customers, who should not leave the premises without it.

Tipping

A tip is generally given even where service is included *(servizio compreso)*. Hotel staff, waiters, taxi drivers, hairdressers and tour guides all expect to be tipped.

Opening Times

Shops are open Monday to Saturday from 8, 8.30 or 9am–12, 12.30 or 1pm and from around 3.30pm to roughly 7.30pm. Many shops close on Monday morning and Thursday afternoon. Museum opening times vary considerably; check the text for details of each one. Churches tend to close at lunchtime (noon onwards), like the rest of the country.

Filling stations

These also tend to close for lunch, like most of the rest of Italy; cash-operated filling stations run on 10,000-lire notes. For filling stations remaining open at night, consult the daily papers.

Post

The Posta Centrale (main post office, open daily 8.25am–7.40pm) is on the Piazza San Silvestro; smaller post offices are open Monday to Friday 8.25am–1.50pm, Saturday 8.25–11.50am. Stamps *(francobolli)* can also be purchased from tobacconists *(tabacchi)*. Postcards and letters with Vatican stamps must be posted from blue Vatican post-boxes.

Public telephone for token calls

Telephoning

This can be done from public telephones, either with *gettoni* (phone tokens) or with 100-, 200- and 500-lire coins; phone cards *(carta telefonica)* are also available and can

99

be bought at tobacconists. Bars and shops with a yellow dialling symbol in their windows also have public phones. The official telephone office, SIP, is separate from the post office in Italy; here you can dial long-distance calls yourself and pay afterwards. The SIP offices on the Piazza San Silvestro and at the main station are open 24 hours, and the one on the Corso Vittorio Emanuele is open from 8am–9.30pm. Dialling codes: Australia 61; France 33; Germany 49; Japan 81; Netherlands 31; Spain 34; United Kingdom 44; US and Canada 1. AT&T:172-1011, Sprint: 172-1877 (note: public phones may require coin or card.)

Time
Italy is six hours ahead of US Eastern Standard Time and one hour ahead of Greenwich Mean Time.

Voltage
Within Rome 220v, outside Rome 110–220v. Safety plugs cannot always be used. Specialist electrical shops can provide adaptors.

Public Holidays
1 January (New Year); 6 January (Epiphany, or *befana*); Easter Monday; 25 April (Liberation Day); 1 May (Labour Day); Ascension; 15 August (Assumption of the Virgin, or *ferragosto*); 1 November (All Saints' Day); 8 December (the Immaculate Conception); 25/26 December (Christmas). On the evening of 21 April each year the Capitoline Hill is illuminated to celebrate the legendary foundation of the city.

Shopping by trolley

Swimming

The Mediterranean (Tyrrhenian Sea) is just 25km (15 miles) away from Rome. The most popular beaches – since they can be comfortably reached by Metro – are at Ostia and Castel Fusano. There is a nudist beach (with plenty of sand-dunes) near Capocotta.

Several beaches further to the south are highly recommended, between Anzio and Cap Circe, and the Lago di Bracciano is also good (38km/23 miles northwest of Rome, *see page 79*). The Bagni di Tivoli have been famous since antiquity for their sulphur springs, the Acqua Albule.

Medical

Visitors from the EC have the right to claim health services available to Italians. UK visitors should obtain Form E111 from the Department of Health prior to departure.

Addresses of chemists open at night and phone numbers of emergency medical services are usually listed in the daily papers.

Embassies will be happy to give you details of English-speaking doctors.

Pharmacy

Theft

Keep a careful eye on your property – theft is the order of the day. Documents and valuables should be kept in hotel safes, and it's advisable to take your radio with you when leaving your car. Beware, too, of beggars: do not allow them to get too close to you, as they may turn out to be pick-pockets as well.

The main emergency numbers (police, medical assistance) all over Italy are 112 and 113; for emergency breakdown services, dial 116; for the fire brigade in Rome, dial 115; and for the ambulance service, dial 5100.

Lost and found

The City of Rome, its transport authority and also the main station (Stazione Termini) each maintain their own Lost Property Offices:

Ufficio del Comune di Roma, Via Bettoni 1, Monday to Saturday 9am–1pm.

Ufficio del ATAC, Via Volturno 65, Monday to Saturday 10am–1pm.

Ufficio di Stazione Termini, Monday to Saturday 8am–4pm.

Consulates

Canada: Via Zara 30, tel: 8441841
Ireland: Largo Nazareno 3, tel: 6782541
UK: Via XX Settembre 80a, tel: 834194
USA: Via Vittorio Veneto 121, tel: 46741

Balcony rooms with street views

Accommodation

Hotels *(alberghi)* in Rome are officially classed into five categories: luxury hotels *$$$$$*; category I *$$$$*; category II *$$$*; category III *$$*; and category IV *$*. Boarding-houses *(pensioni)* are subdivided into three categories and are usually just as good as hotels. A list of hotels and boarding-houses showing the different prices can be obtained from tourist offices abroad or in Rome. Prices within different categories can vary greatly. A simple single bed-room can be obtained for as little as 60,000 lire, while a luxury suite can cost up to 500,000 lire. The following selection (not based on quality) contains a few hotels from each category in the centre of Rome:

$$$$$ **Ambasciatori Palace**, Via Vittorio Veneto 70; **Bernini Bristol** Piazza Barberine 23; **Hassler-Villa Medici**, Piazza Trinità dei Monti 6; **Eden**, Via Ludovisi 49; **Le Grand Hotel**, Via Vittorio E Orlando; **Excelsior**, Via Vittorio Veneto 125; **Lord Byron**, Via G de Notaris 5; **Minerva**, Piazza Santa Maria sopra Minerva; **Raphael**, Largo Febo 2.

Old hotels have stone portals

$$$$ **De la Ville**, Via Sistina 69; Jolly, Corso d'Italia 1; **Regina Hotel Baglioni**, Via Vittorio Veneto 72; **Majestic**, Via Vittorio Veneto 50; **Mediterraneo**, Via Cavour 15; **Sole al Pantheon**, Via del Pantheon 63. **Plaza Hotel**, Via del Corso 126.

$$$ **Della Torre Argentina**, Corso Vittorio Emanuele 102; **Arcangelo**, Via Boezio 15; **Carriage**, Via delle Carrozze 36; **Condotti**, Via Mario de'Fiori 37; **Della Conciliazione**, Borgo Pio 164; **Gregoriana**, Via Gregoriana 18; **Adriano**, Via di Pallacorda 2; **Madrid**, Via Mario

de'Fiori 93; **Gerber**, Via degli Scipioni 241; **Britannia**, Via Napoli 64; **Diana**, Via Principe Amadeo 4; Nord-Nuova Roma, Via Amendola 3; **Sitea**, Via Vittorio Emanuele Orlando 90; **Colosseum**, Via Sforza 10; **Marcella**, Via Flavia 104; **Edera**, Via Piliziano 75; **Genio**, Via Zanardelli 28.

$$ **Fabrello-White**, Via Vittoria Colonna 11; **Portoghesi**, Via dei Portoghesi 1; **Margutta**, Via Laurina 34; **Igea**, Via Principe Amadeo 97; **Alba**, Leonina 12; **Baltic**, Via XX Settembre 89; **Campo Marzio**, Via Campo Marzio 7; **Forti's Guest House**, Via Cosseria 2; **Smeraldo**, Via dei Chiodaroli 11; **Suisse**, Via Gregoriana 56; **Trinità dei Monti**, Via Sistina 91; **Sole**, Via del Biscione 76; **Campo de'Fiori**, Via del Biscione 6; **Pensione Barrett**, Largo Argentina 47.

Small hotels are more friendly

Establishments referred to as *locande* (inns) are generally regarded as providing simpler, but clean accommodation; be far more cautious about lodging-houses, referred to as *alloggi*. Prices go up to around 30,000 lire per person.

Youth Hostels

Ostello del Foro Italico (youth hostel), Viale delle Olimpiadi 61; **Casa Internazionale dello Studente 'CIVISO'** (international student home), Viale Ministero degli Affari Esteri 5; **YWCA** (only women students), Via Cesare Balbo 4; **Ostello Marello,** Via Urbana 50; **Esercito della Salvezza – Centro del Giovane**, Via degli Apuli 41; **Domus Mariae**, Via Aurelia 481 (holiday house); **Domus Pacis**, Via Torre Rossa 94 (holiday house).

Camping

Capitol - Ostia Antica, Via Castelfusano 45. Has a swimming pool.

Camping Flaminio, Via Flaminia, 2½km (1½ miles) into town from the motorway ring road on the SS 3 Flaminia.

Roma Camping, Via Aurelia exit, 1½km (1 mile) into town off the *Raccordo Anulare* motorway ring.

Anzio: Internazionale Lido dei Pini, Via Ardeatina, 28km (18 miles). Has a swimming pool.

Anzio: Lido delle Ginestre, Lido dei Pini, Via Ardeatina, 28km (18 miles).

Nettuno: Isola Verde, Via Nettunense, 30km (19 miles). In a pine forest.

Santa Marinella: Marinella, Via Aurelia, 66km (41 miles). Right next to the sea.

Alongside youth hostels and campsites, **monasteries** are also cheap places for young people to stay (organise via the Pilgrims' Office, Via della Conciliazione 10).

Index